I0467345

COLOR
Chinese Art

Conceived, Designed, and Illustrated by:

Mrinal Mitra

Series Edited by:

Swarna Mitra & **Malika Mitra**

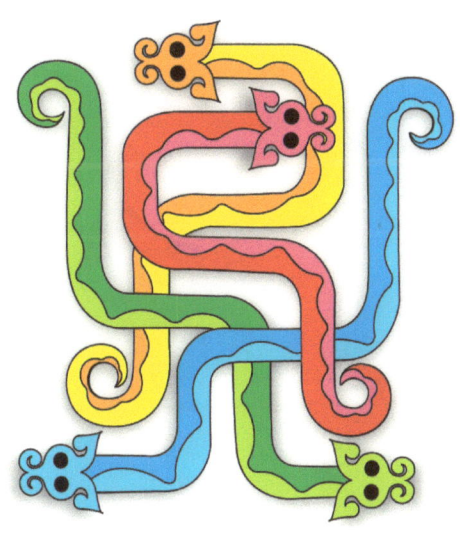

WORLD CULTURE COLORING SERIES

This series is dedicated to the citizens of the world;
from the young blooming minds of children, to the aspired individuals of all ages.

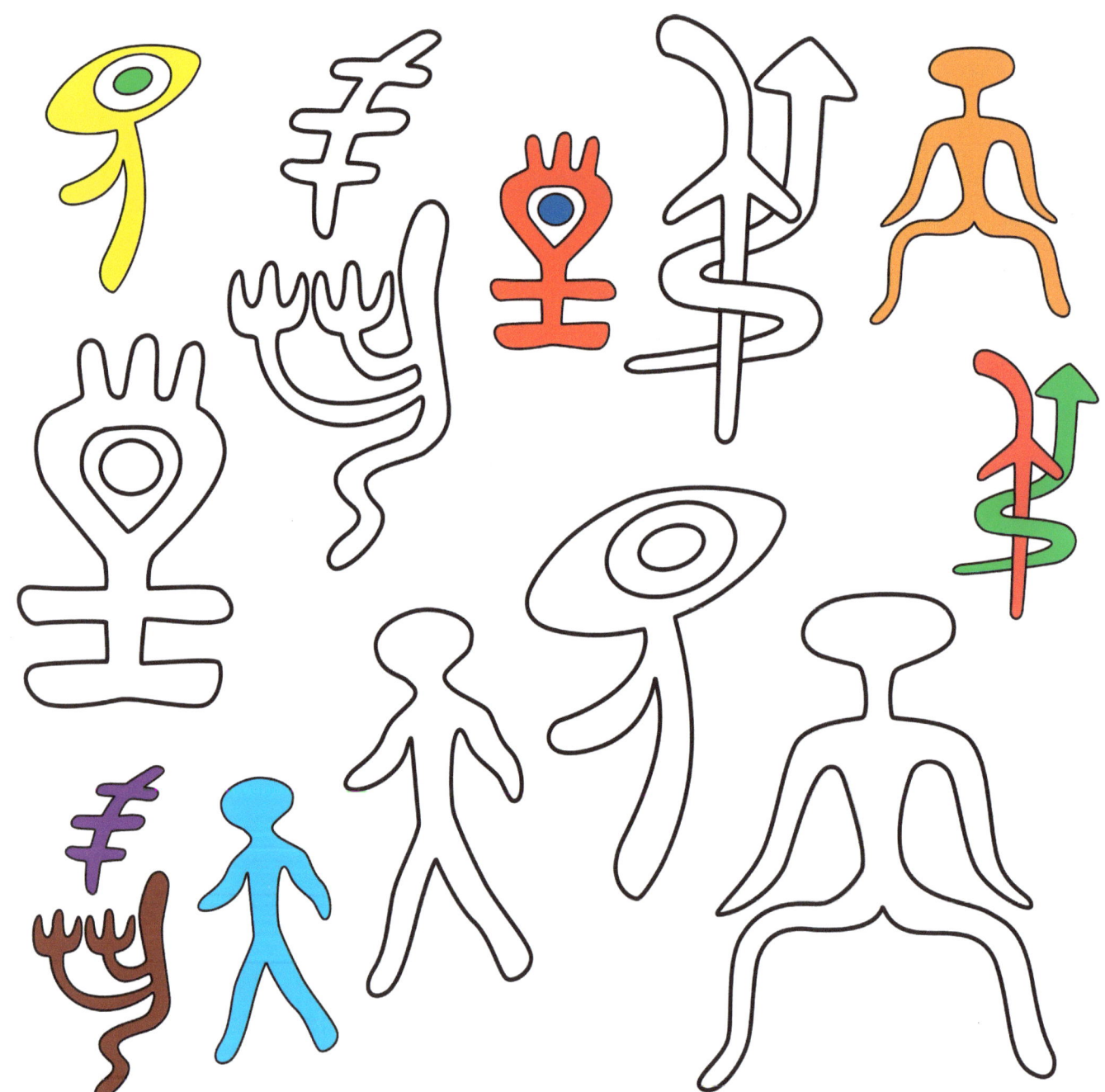

Chinese scripts before standardized in the 3rd Century B.C.E.

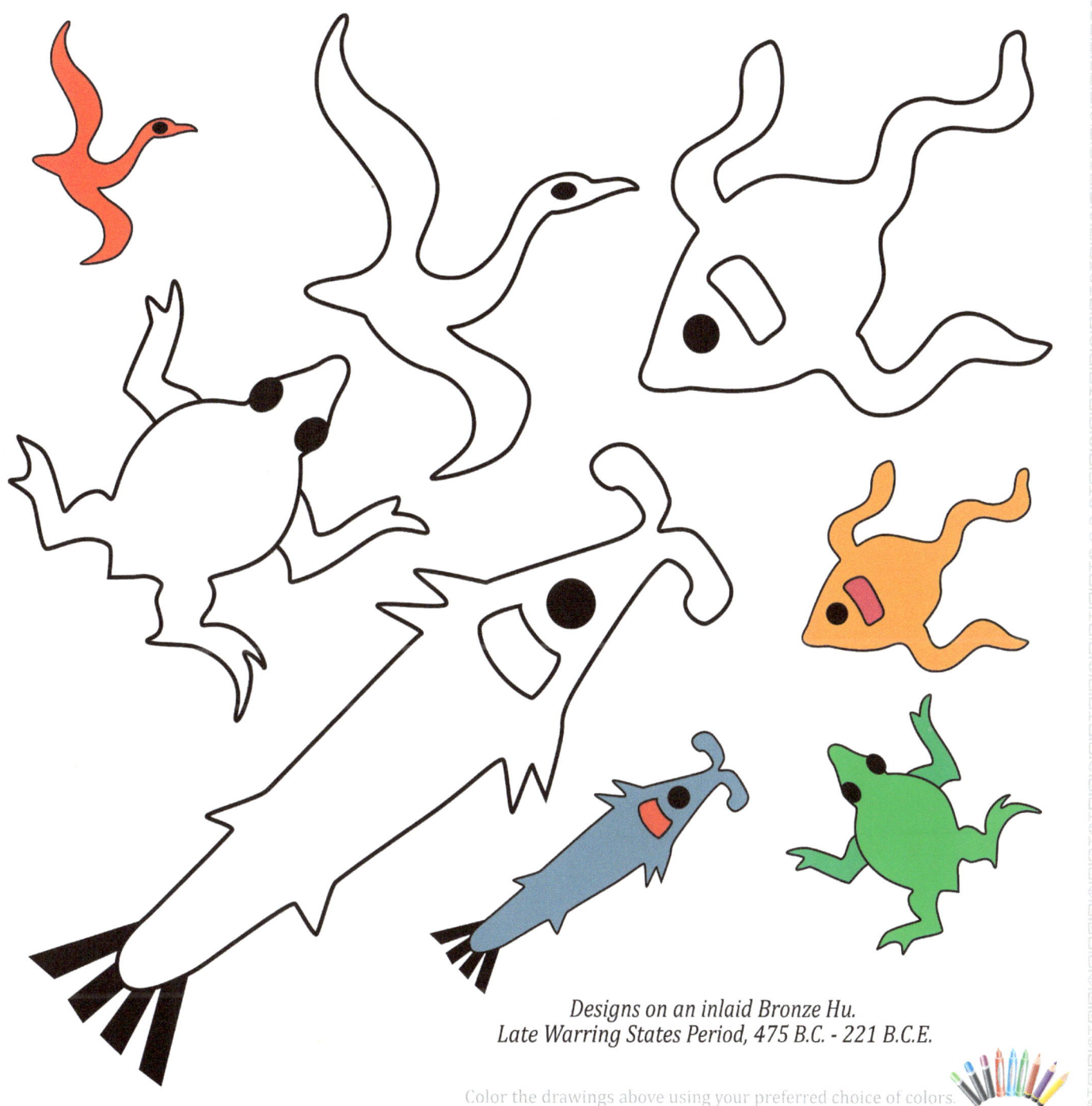

Designs on an inlaid Bronze Hu.
Late Warring States Period, 475 B.C. - 221 B.C.E.

Color the drawings above using your preferred choice of colors.

3

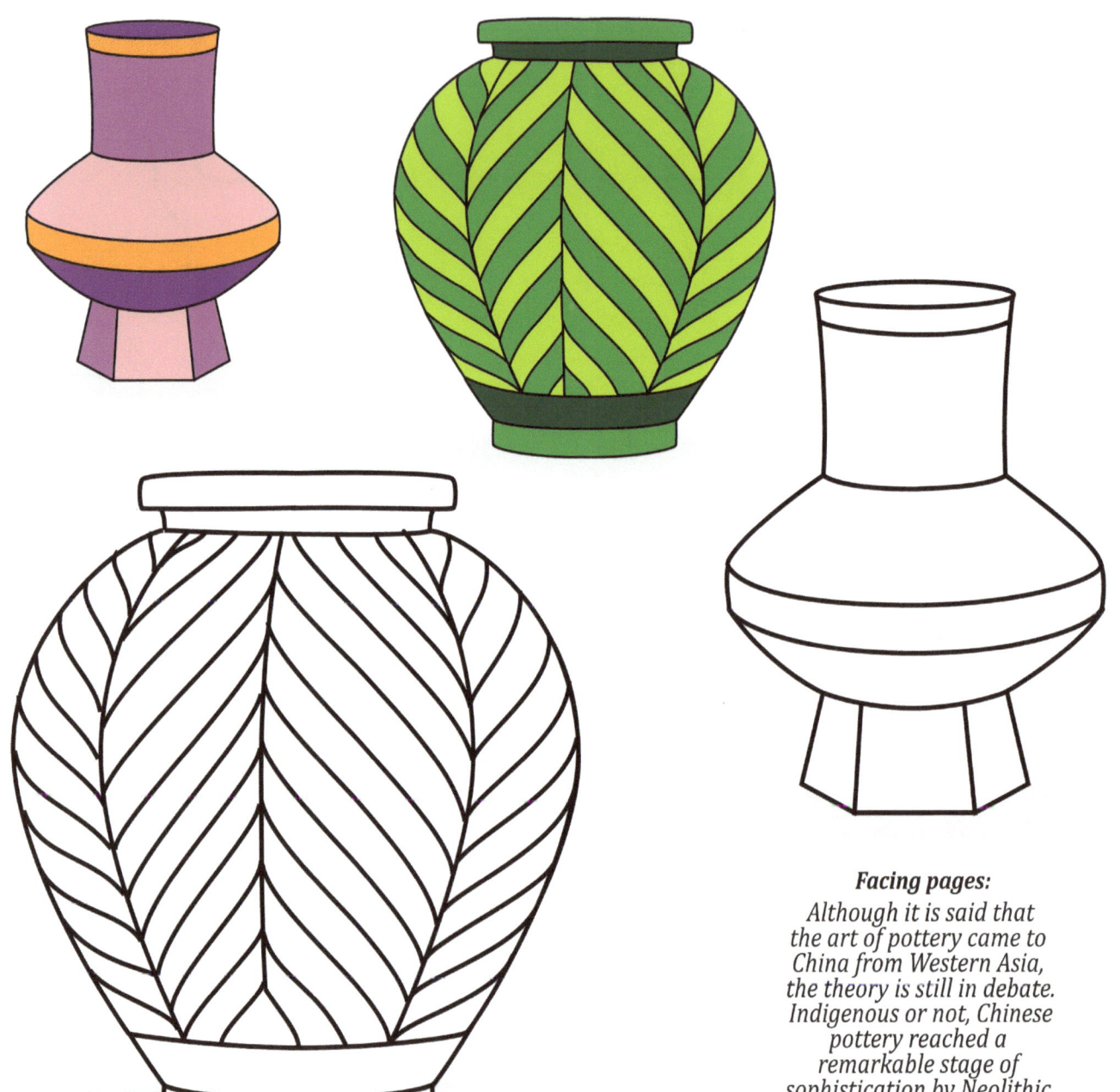

Facing pages:

Although it is said that the art of pottery came to China from Western Asia, the theory is still in debate. Indigenous or not, Chinese pottery reached a remarkable stage of sophistication by Neolithic times. There is no sign of any Stone Age crudity.

Color the drawings above using your preferred choice of colors.

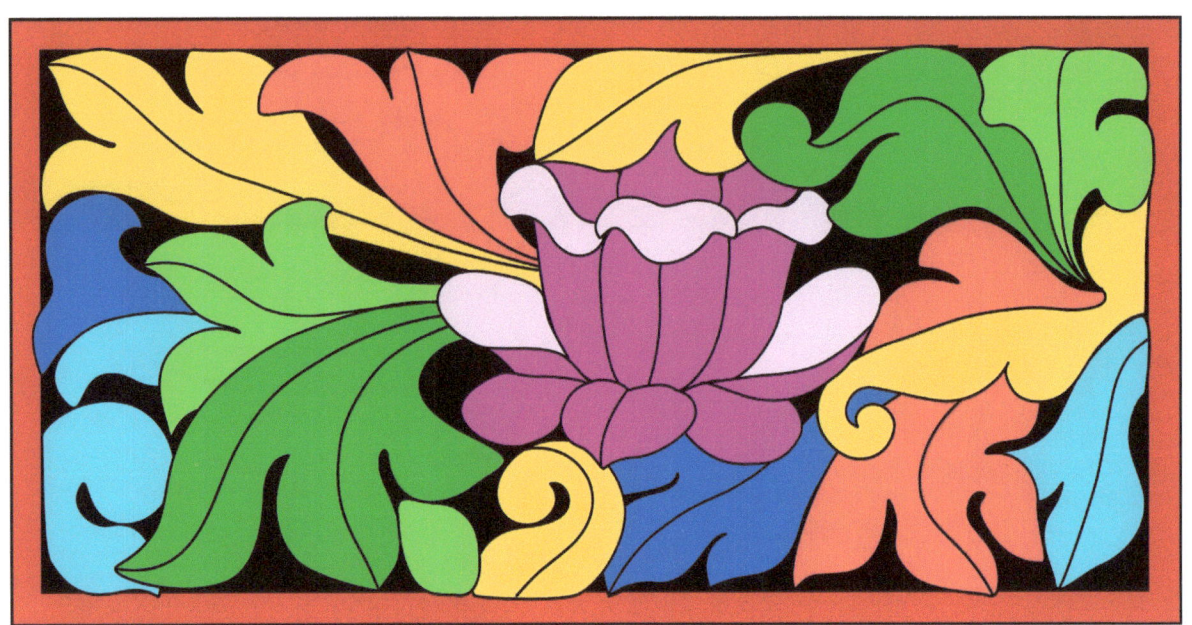

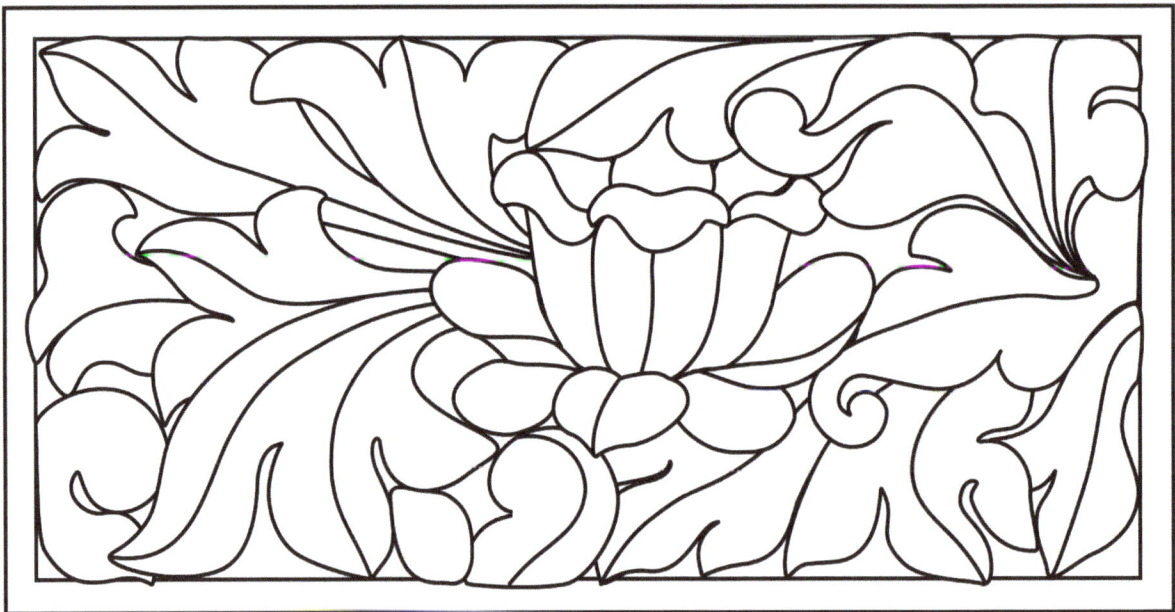

Floral relief work on wall during Shenzong reign. Circa 1000 C.E.

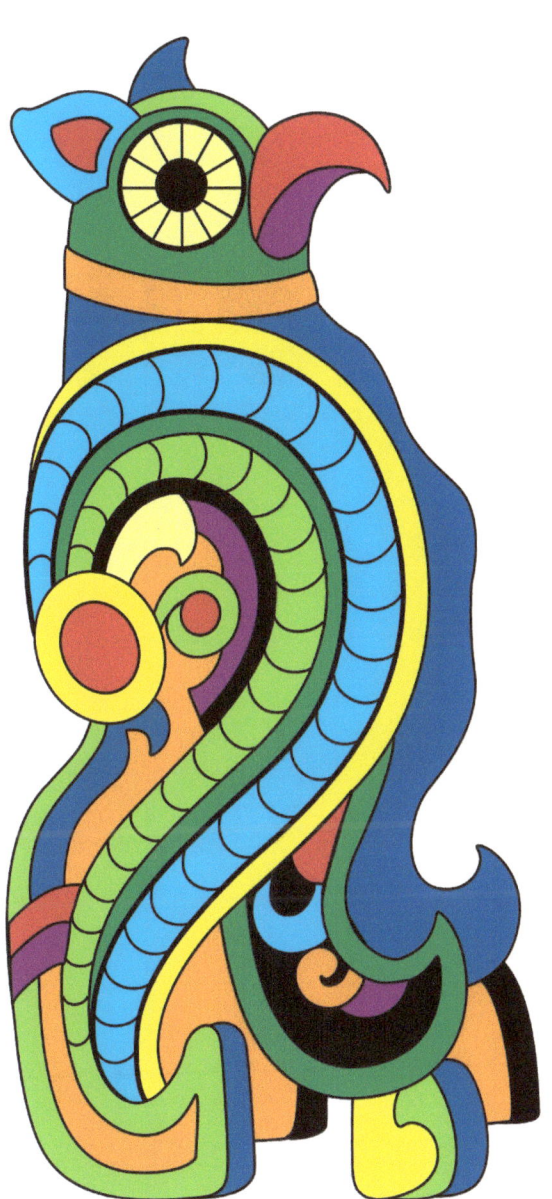
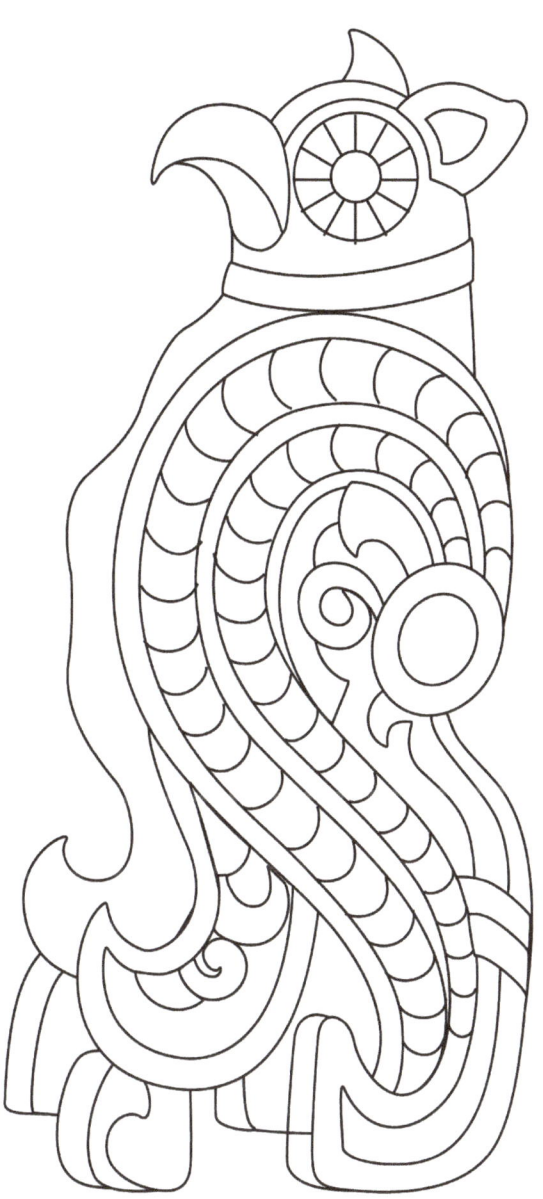

On a Bronze Vessel, Niao - Tsun. After Kwang Chih-Chang.

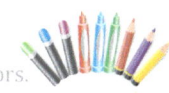

Color the drawings above using your preferred choice of colors.

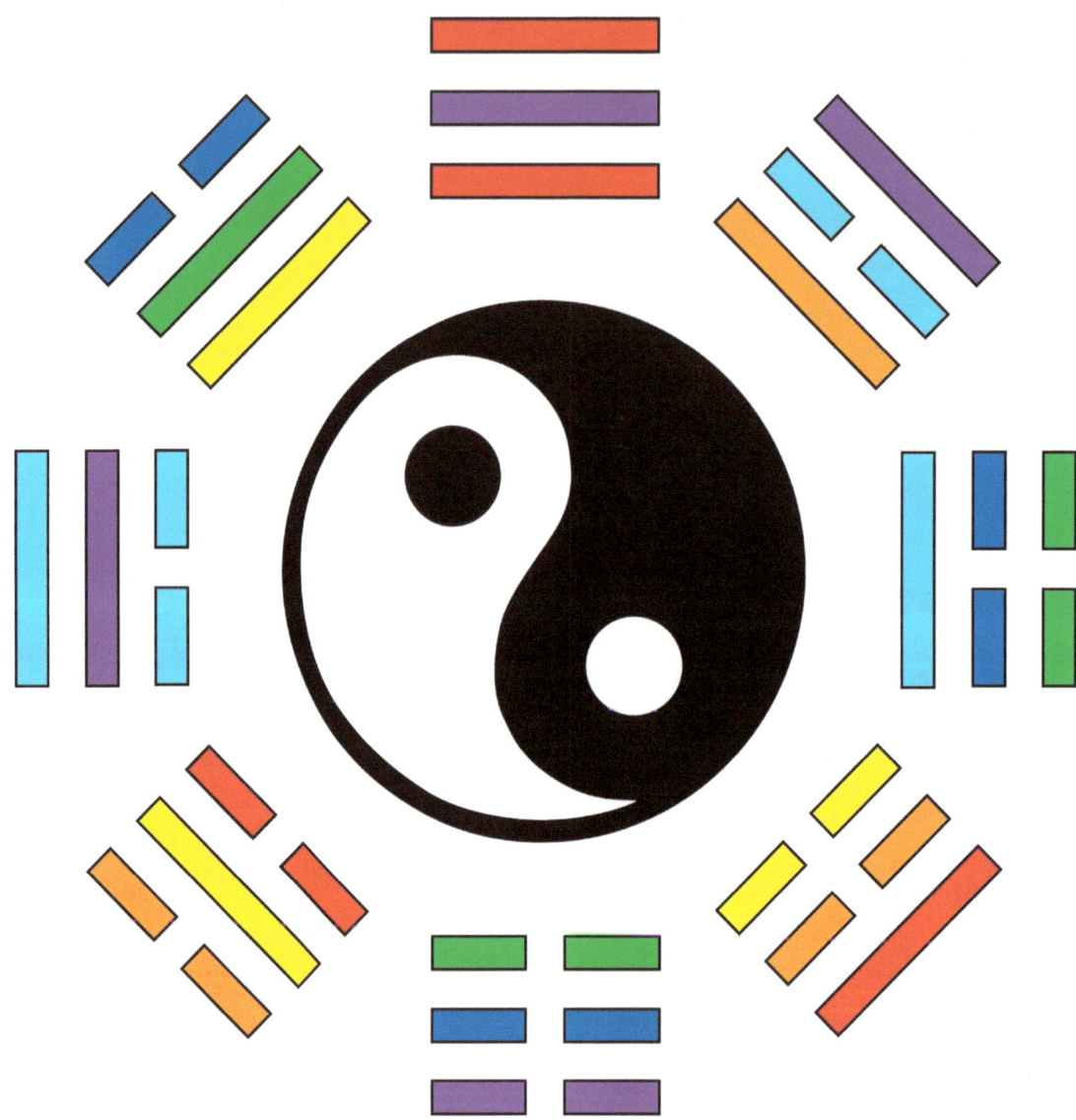

Yin and Yang, Dao Symbol. Daoism called humankind
to follow the natural, cosmic flow of the universe.

Yin and Yang are the prime forces of the universe, surrounded by eight trigrams.
The mystical symbols were viewed as the will of the God. The trigrams are supposedly
discovered by Fu Hsi, the mythical emperor who reigned in 2953 B.C.E.

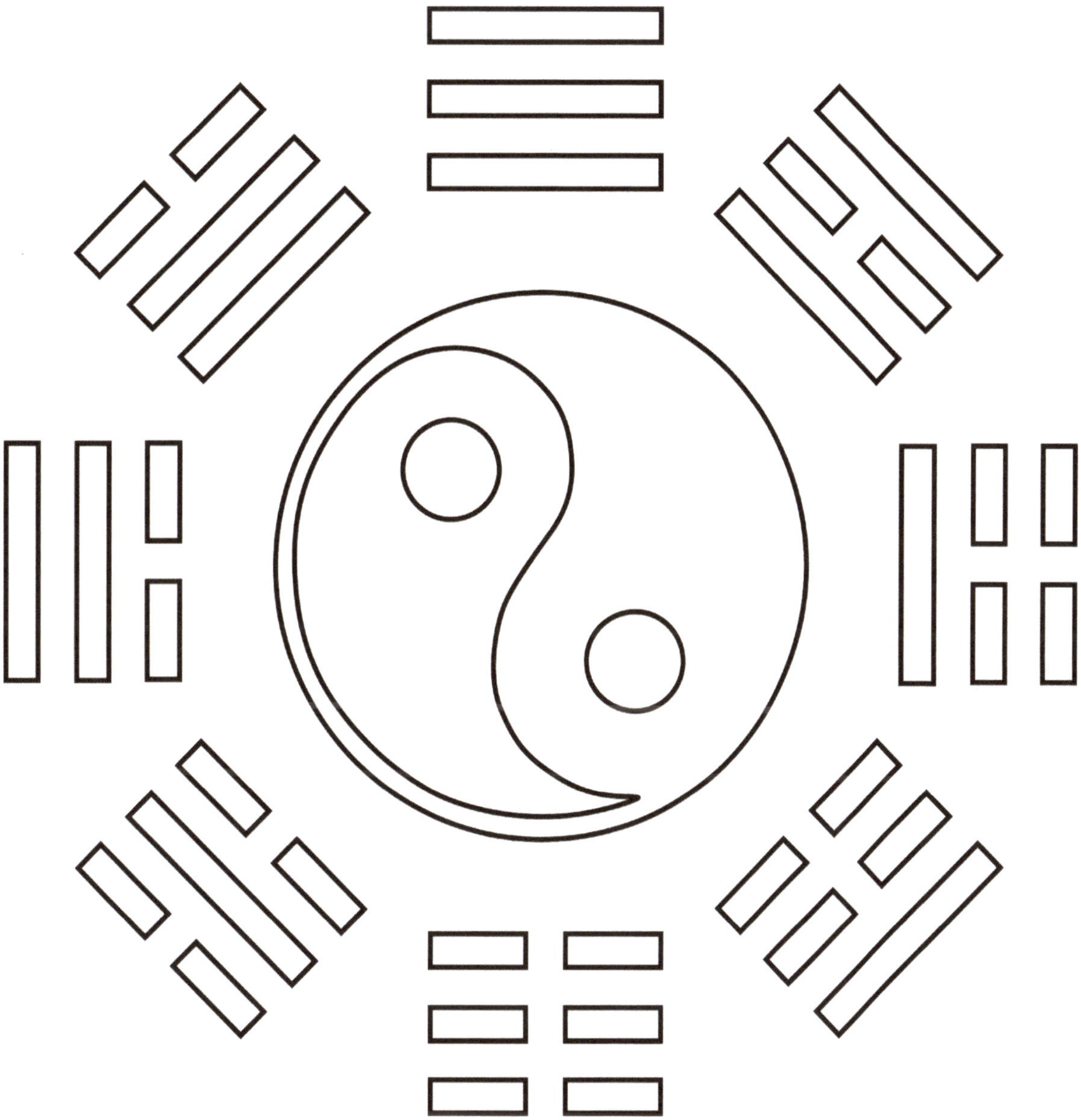

Color the drawing above using your preferred choice of colors.

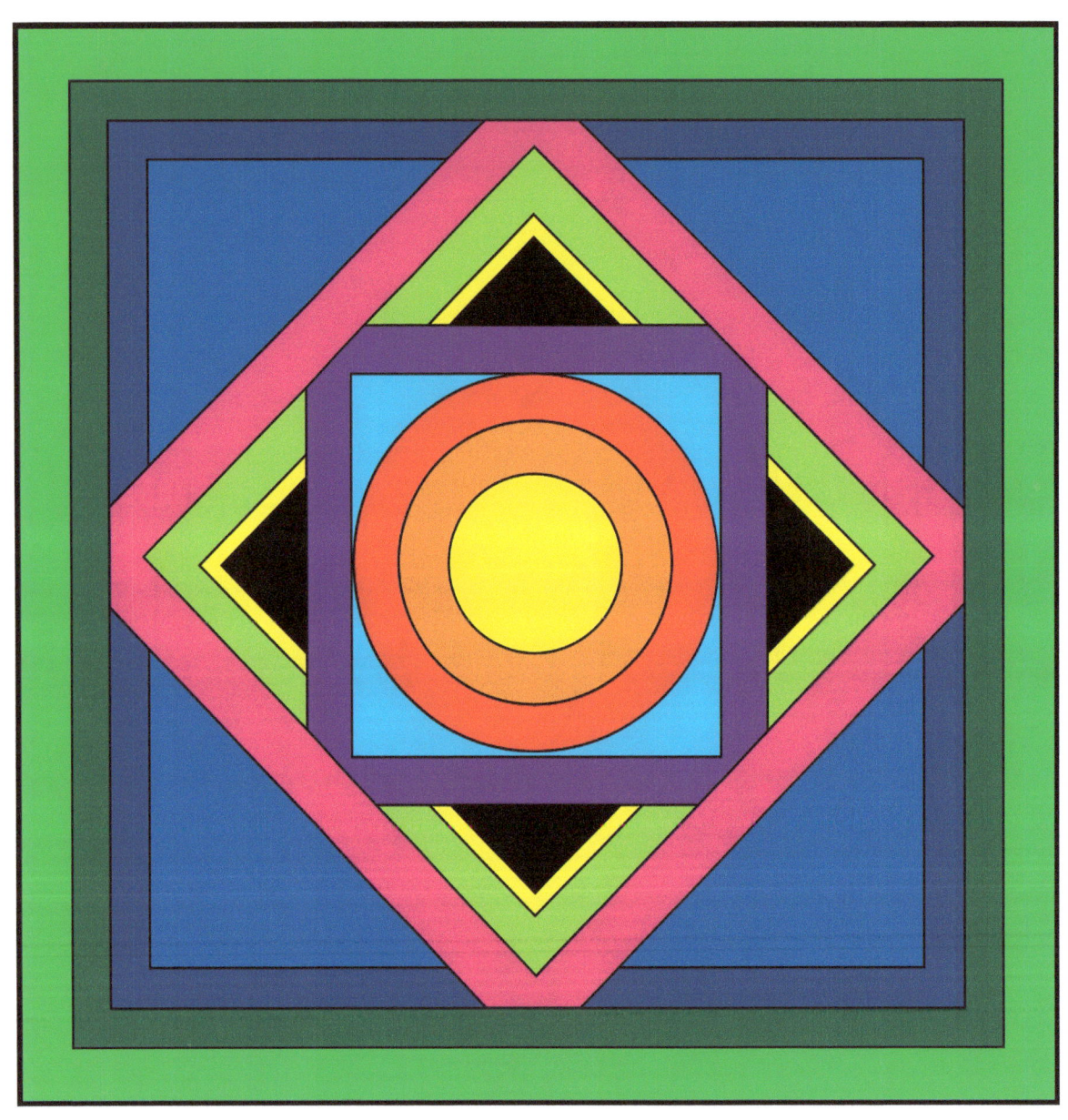

A painting with geometrical shapes on a lower part of a ceiling in Cave Dunhuang. Wei Dynasty, 220 C.E. - 265 C.E.

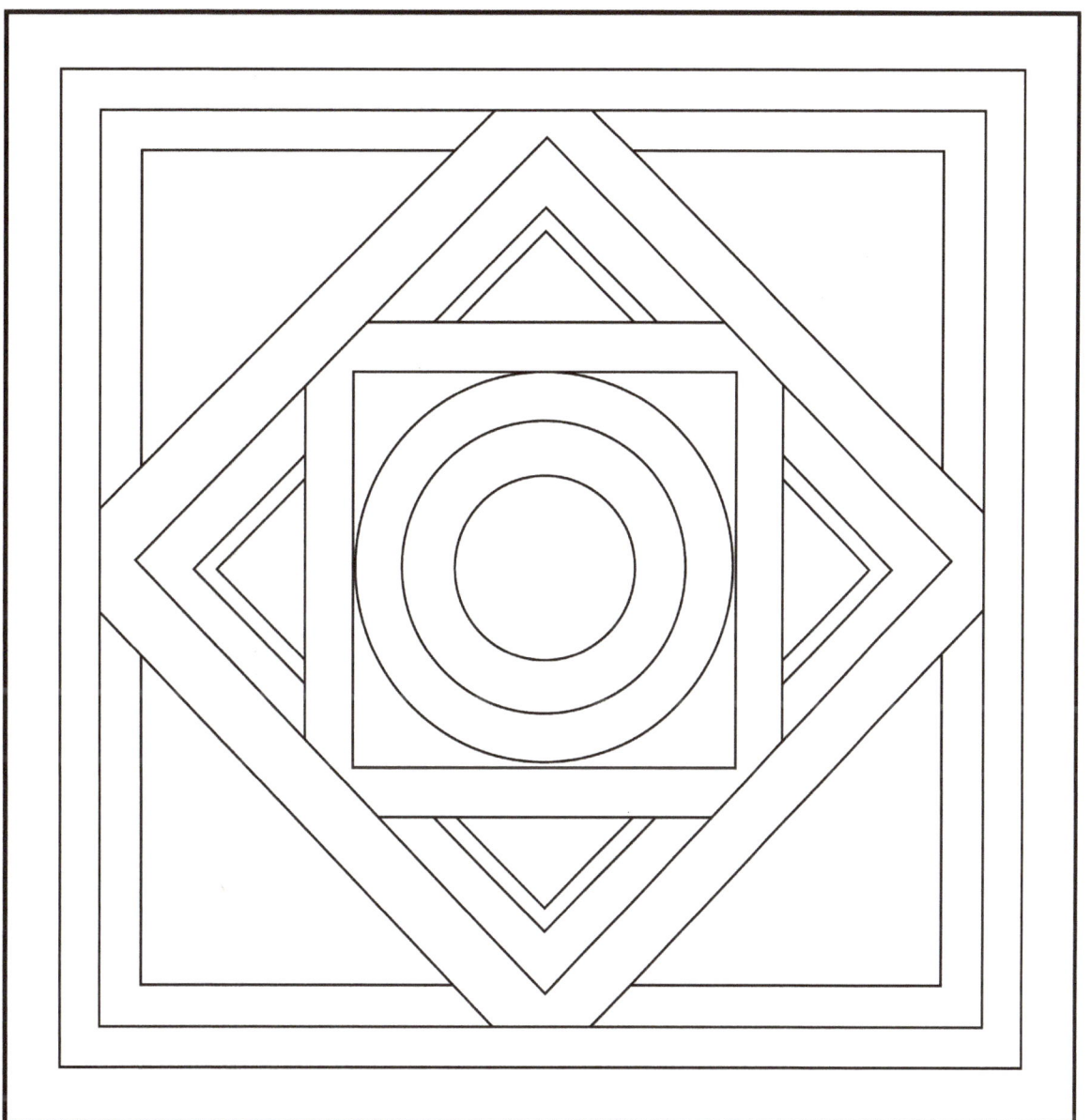

Color the drawing above using your preferred choice of colors.

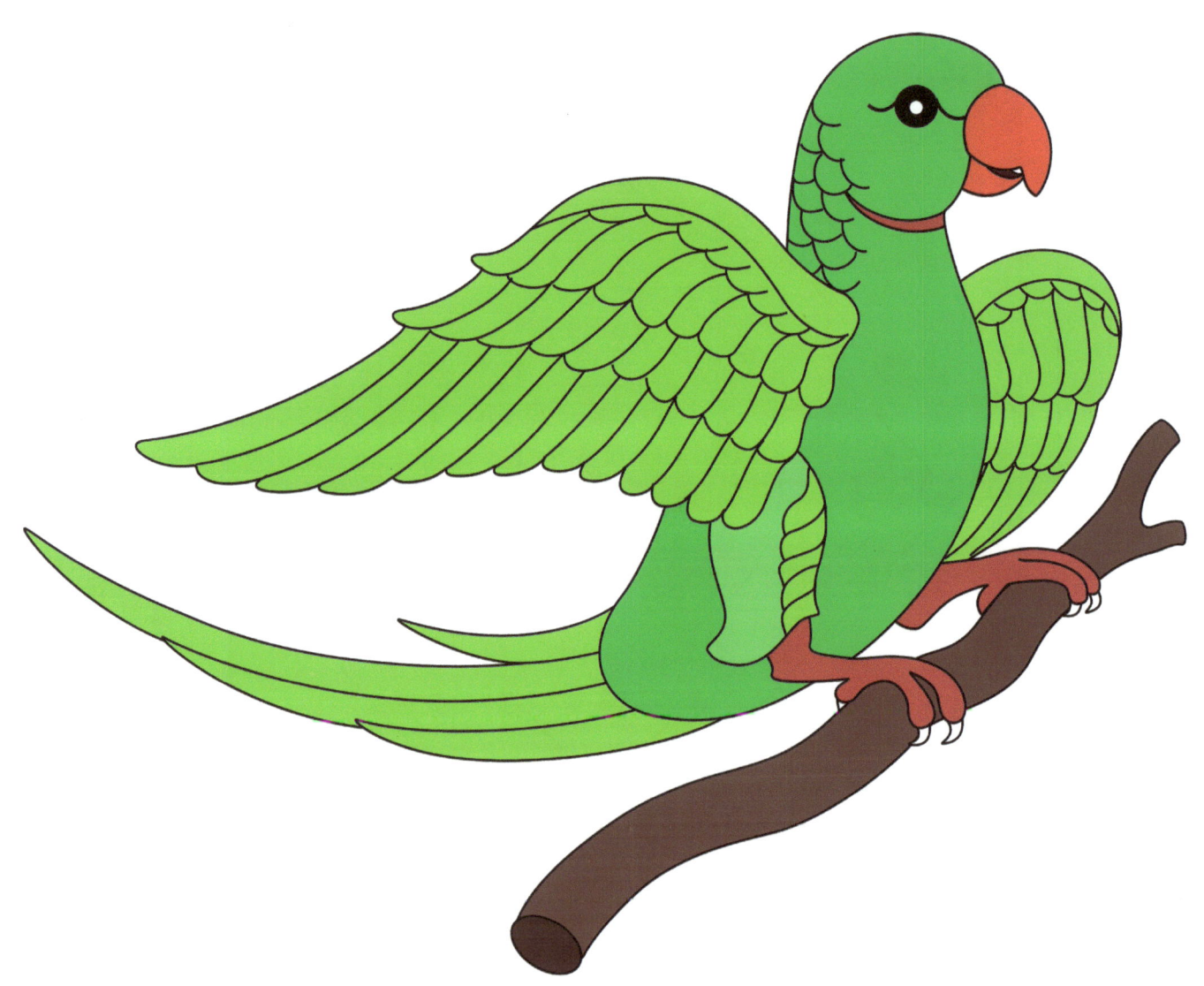

Stylized drawing of a parrot found in a decorated covered jar.
Tang Dynasty, 618 C.E. - 907 C.E.

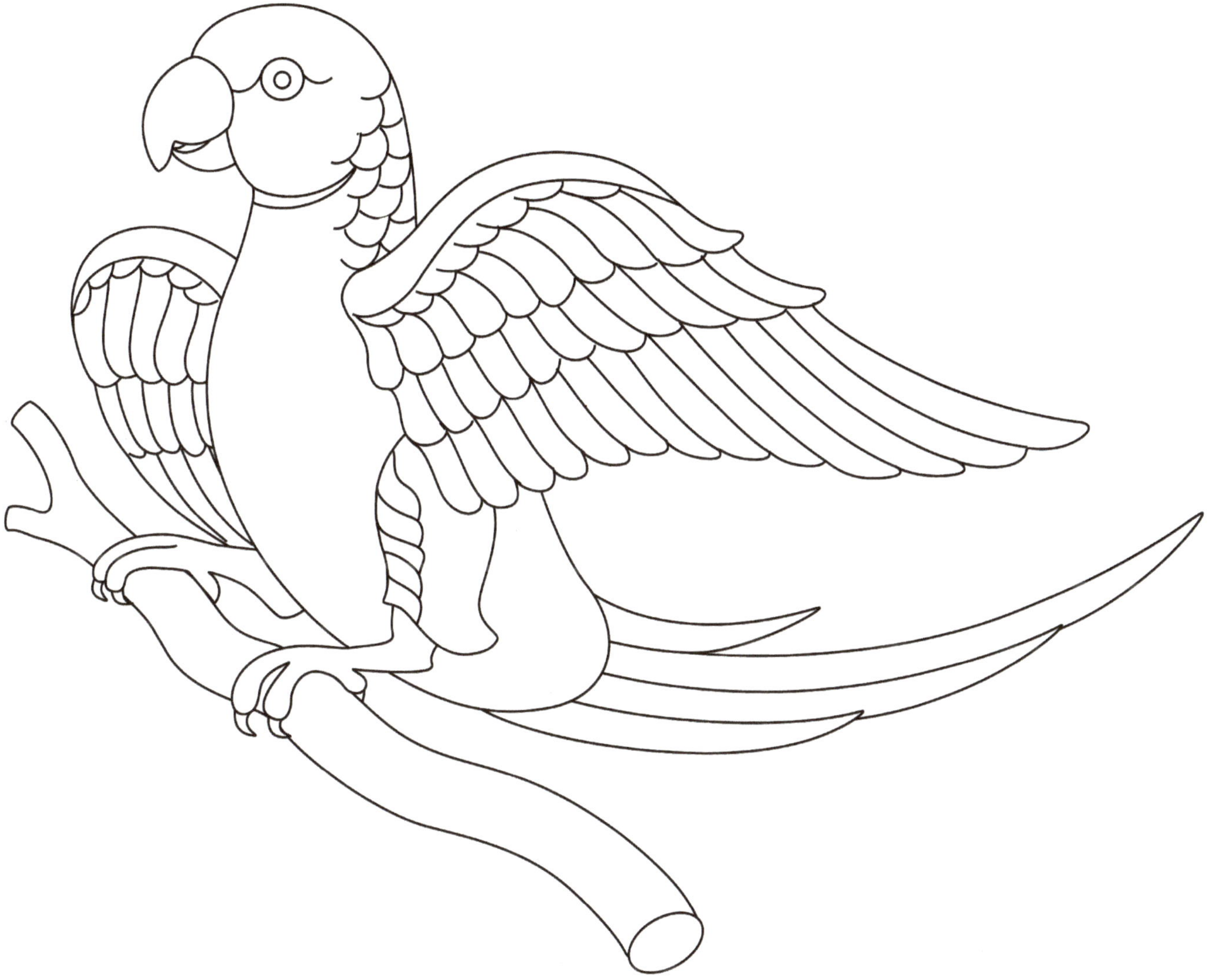

Color the drawing above using your preferred choice of colors.

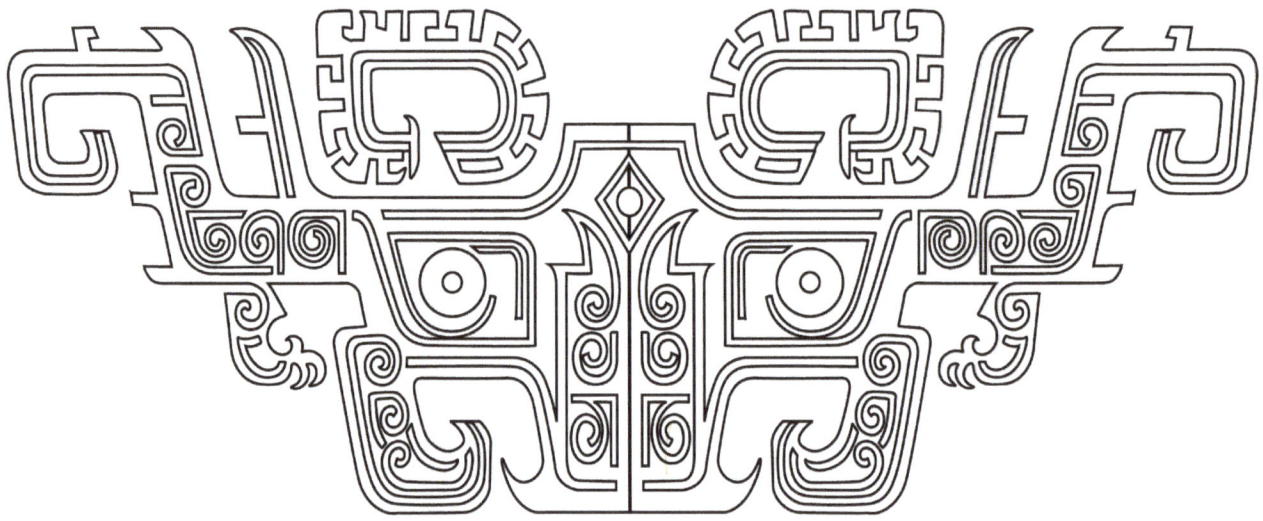

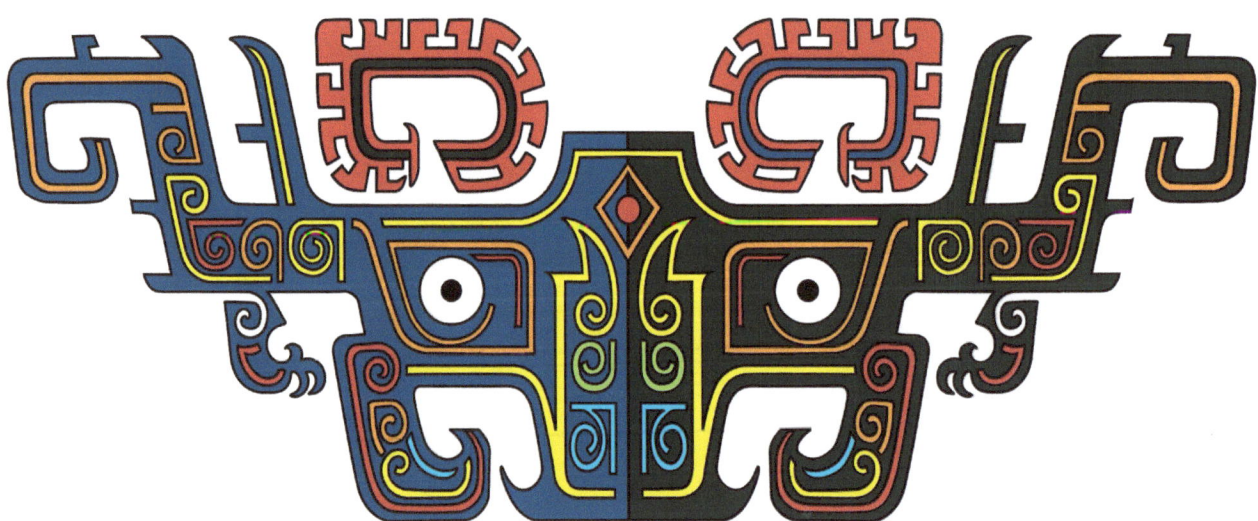

Decoration on Shang Bronzes named "taotic." Shang Dynasty, 1766 - 1121 B.C.E.

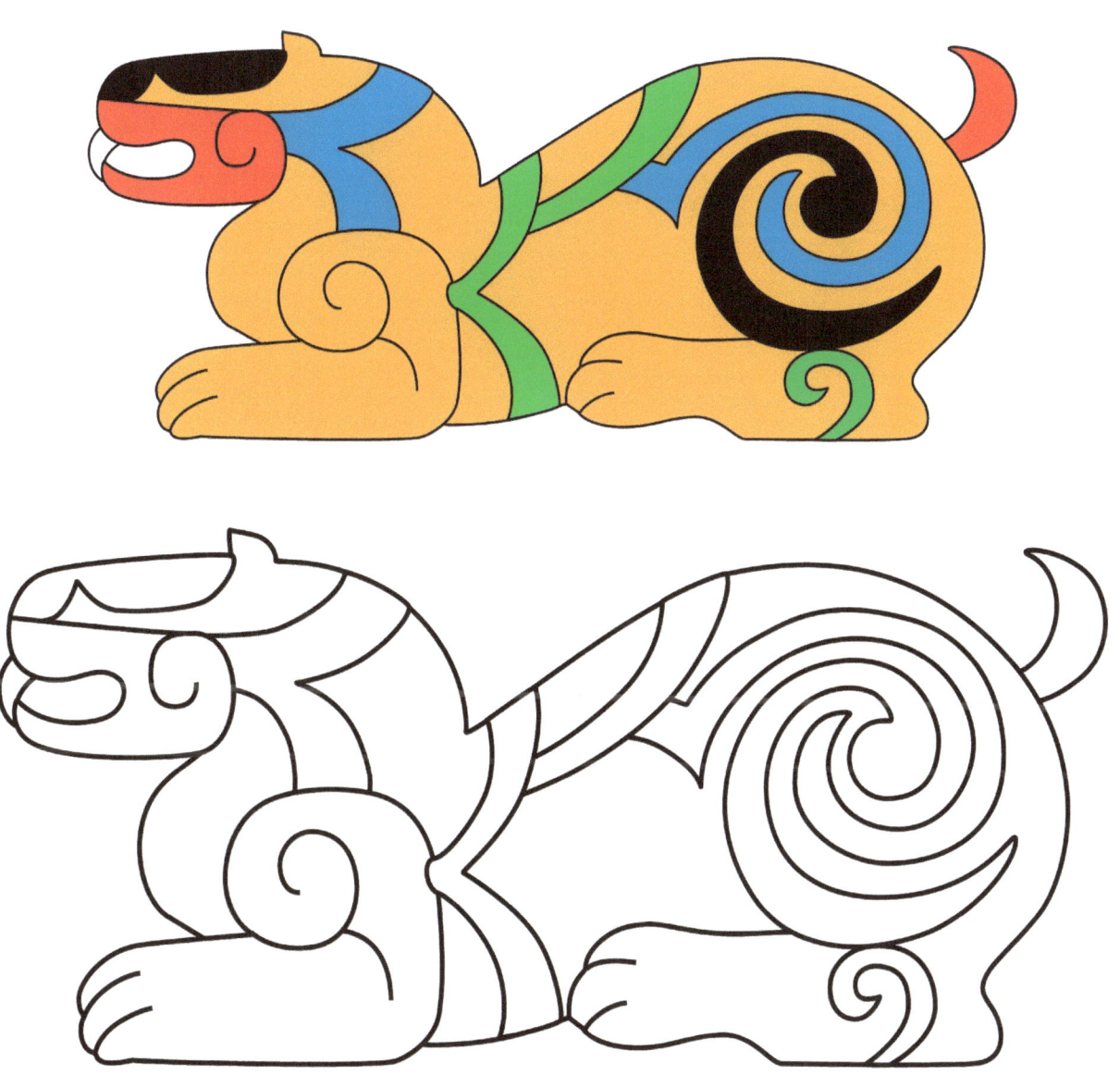

*Stylized animal drawing on a
drum or gong stand. Warring States Period, 475 B.C.E. - 221 B.C.E.*

Color the drawings above using your preferred choice of colors.

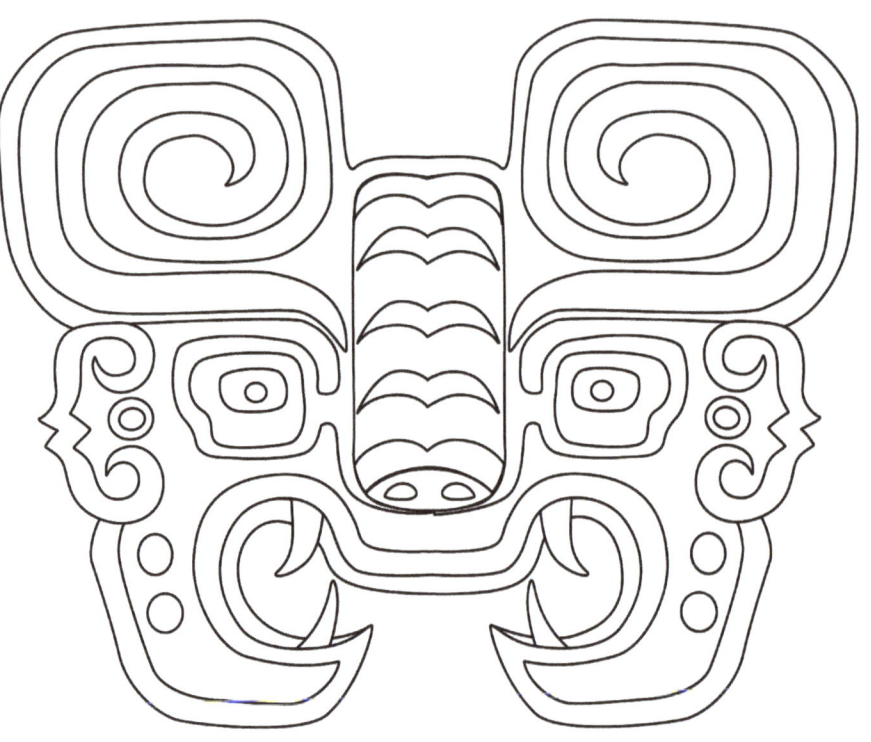

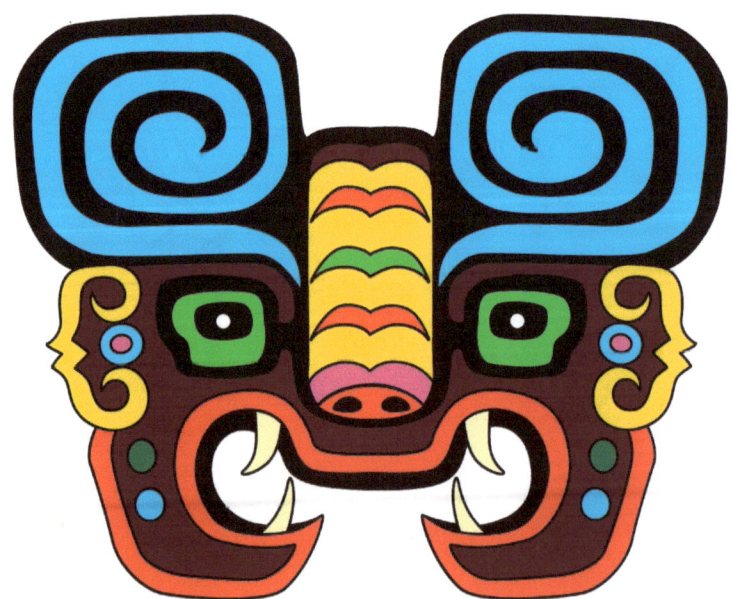

Bronze mask with fangs and horns, worn by the Chinese warriors during 8th Century B.C.E. or earlier.

Chinese Art

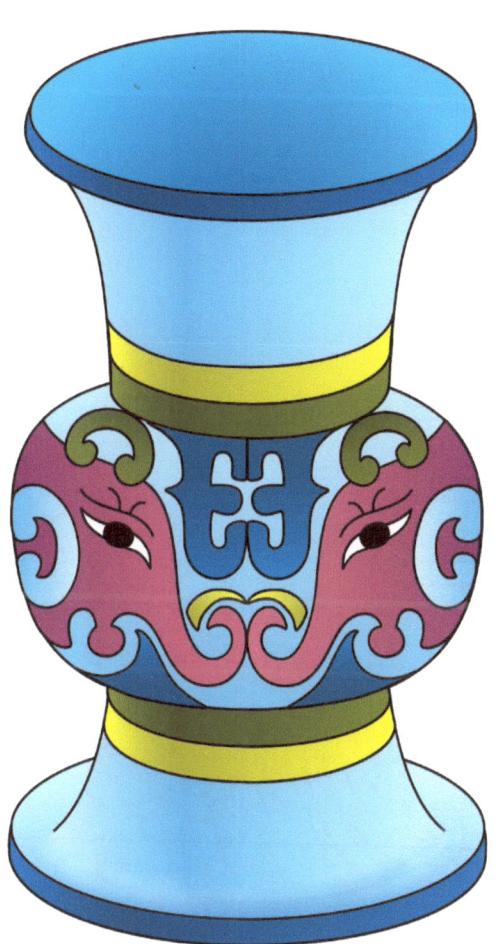

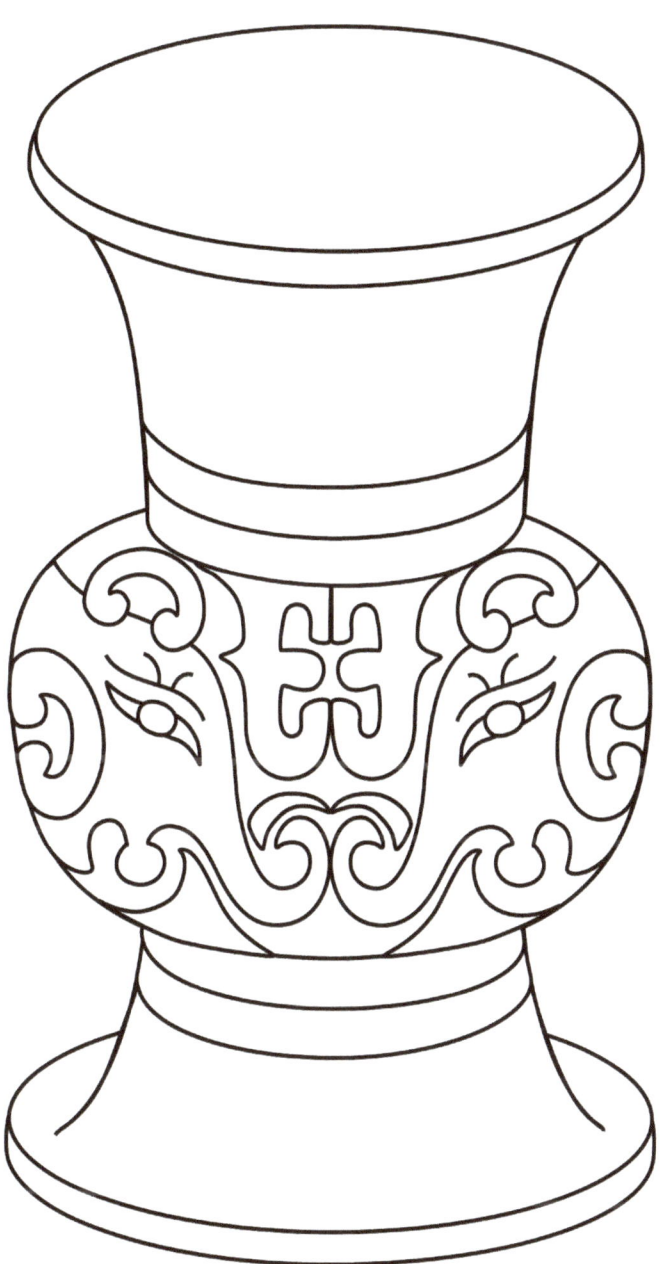

*During the Song Dynasty
(960 C.E. - 1279 C.E.), Scholars avidly
collected and studied Chinese antiquities
made thousands of years earlier.
This bronze wine vessel was one of them.*

Color the drawings above using your preferred choice of colors.

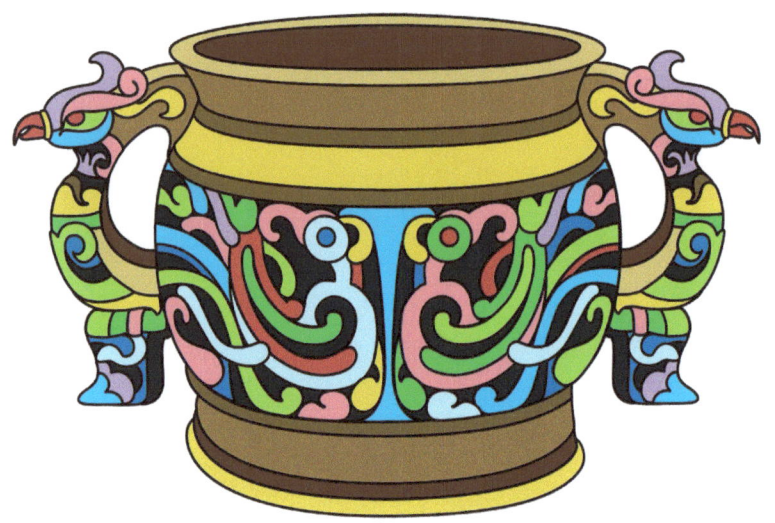

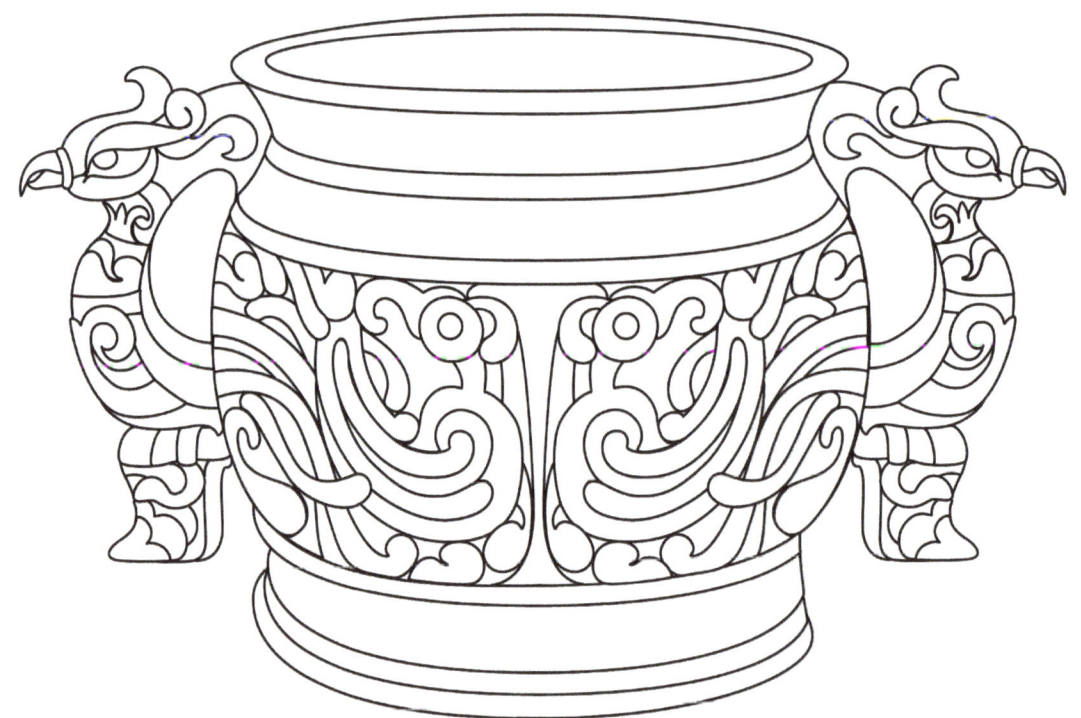

Shang- Zhou Bronze vessel for rituals.

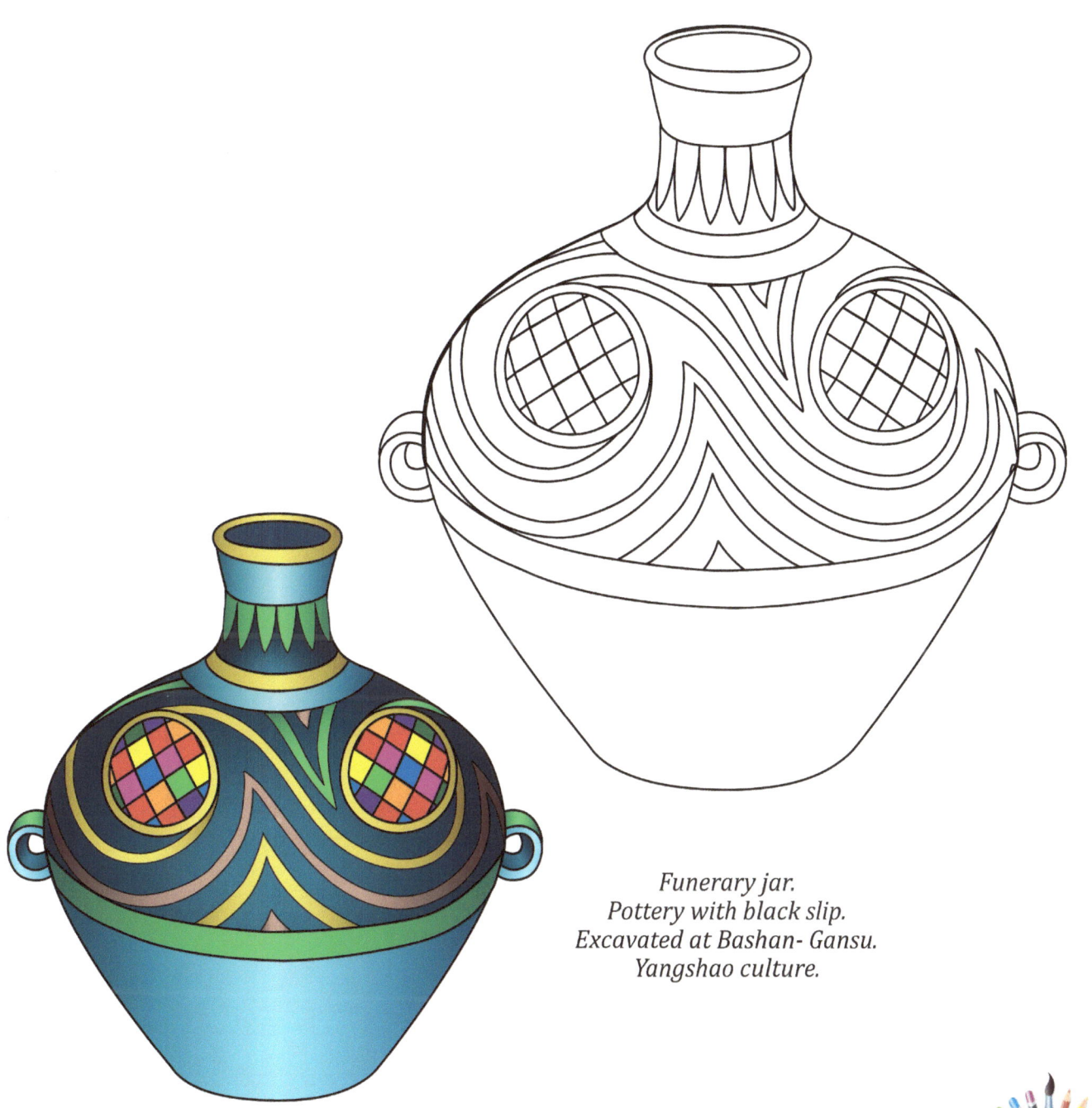

Funerary jar.
Pottery with black slip.
Excavated at Bashan- Gansu.
Yangshao culture.

Color the drawings above using your preferred choice of colors.

19

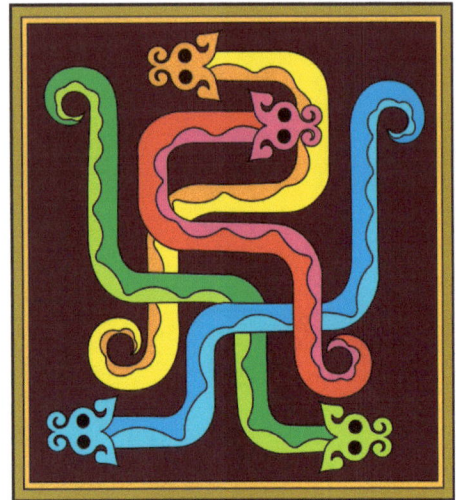

In a Liubo gaming board on stone. Zhongshan royal tomb in Pingshan county. Warring States period, 475 B.C.E. - 221 B.C.E.

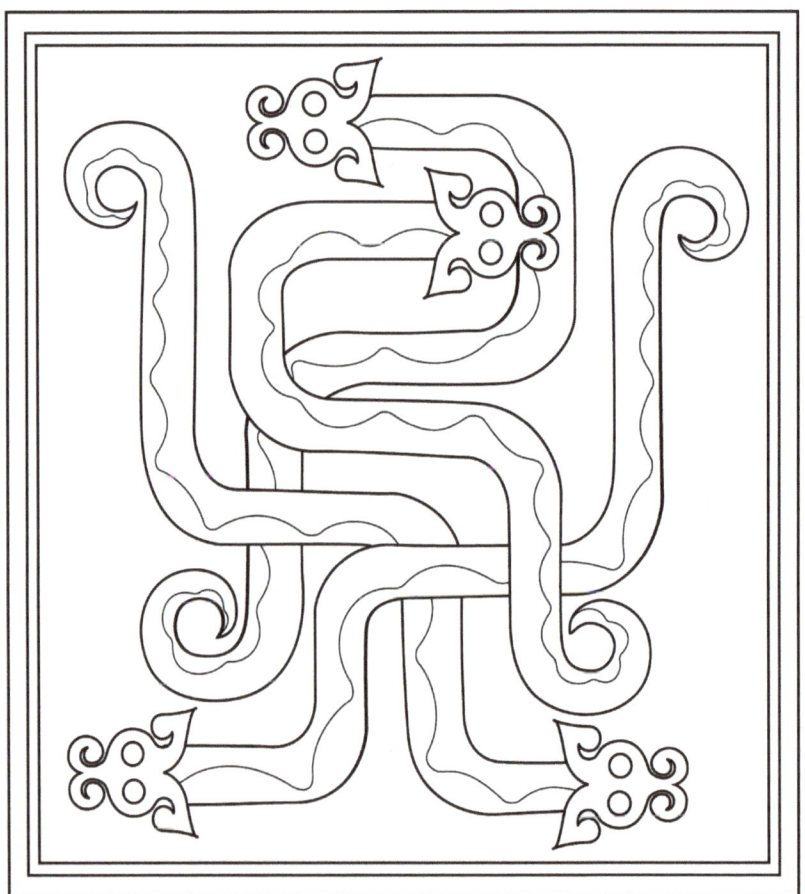

Chinese Art

In a Liubo gaming board on stone.
Zhongshan royal tomb in Pingshan county.
Warring States period, 475 B.C.E. - 221 B.C.E.

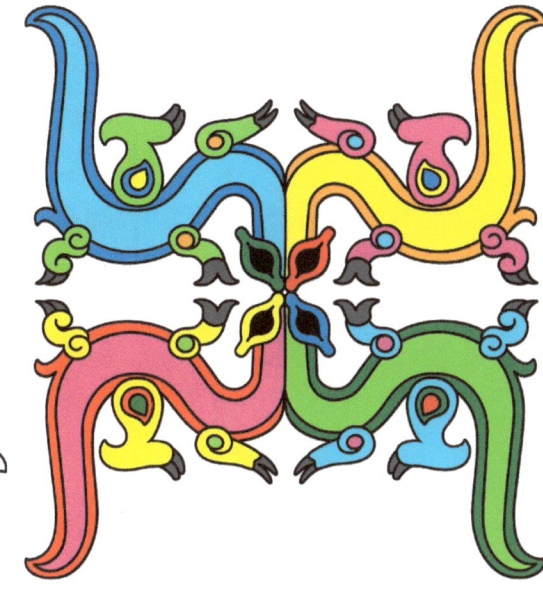

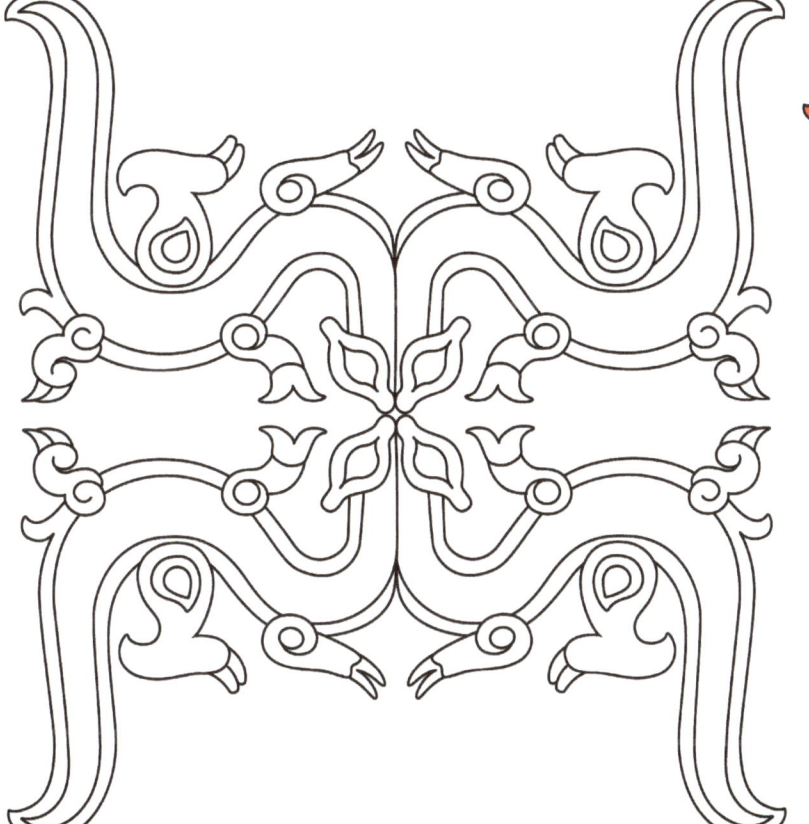

Color the drawings above using your preferred choice of colors.

21

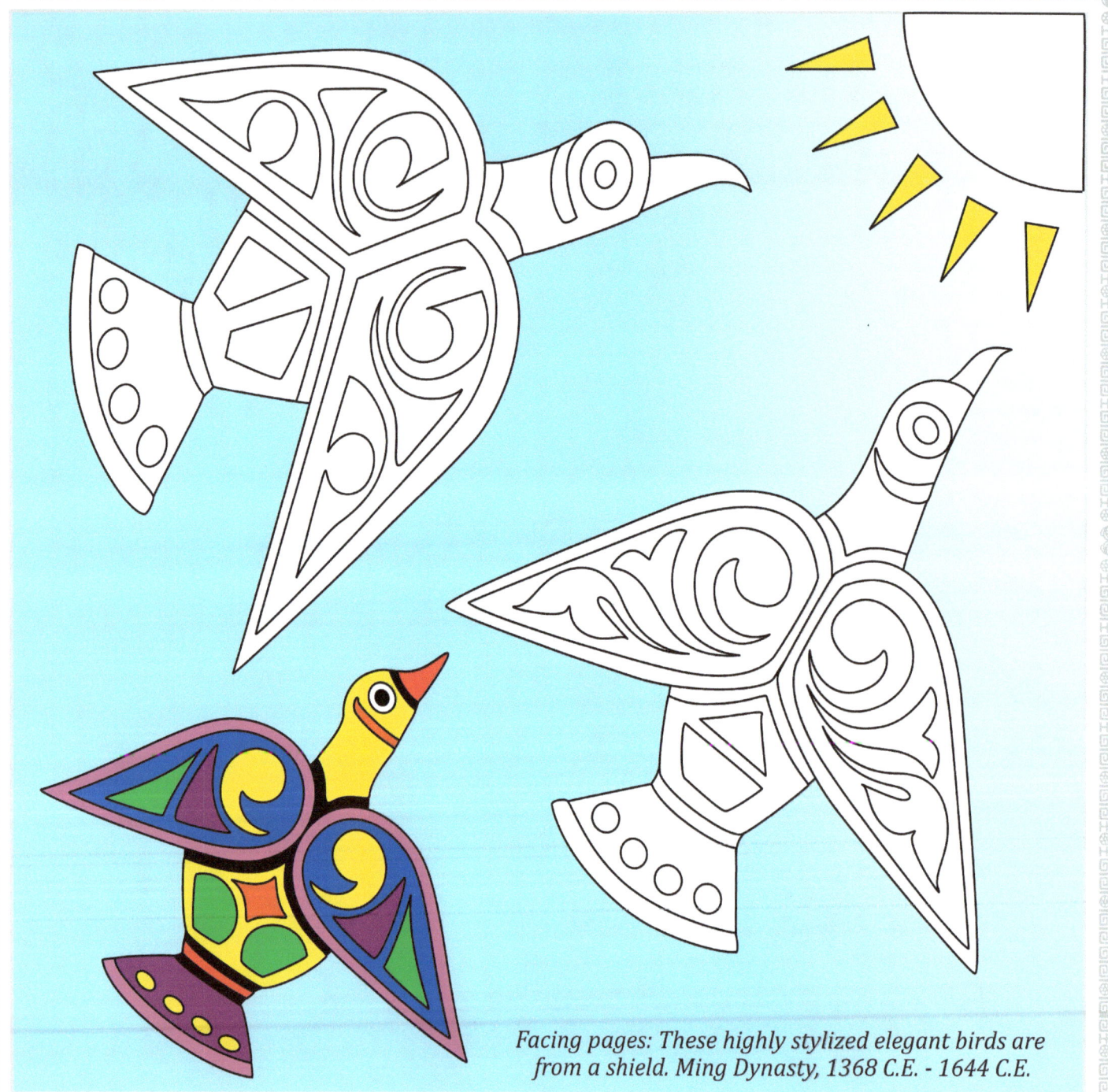

Facing pages: These highly stylized elegant birds are from a shield. Ming Dynasty, 1368 C.E. - 1644 C.E.

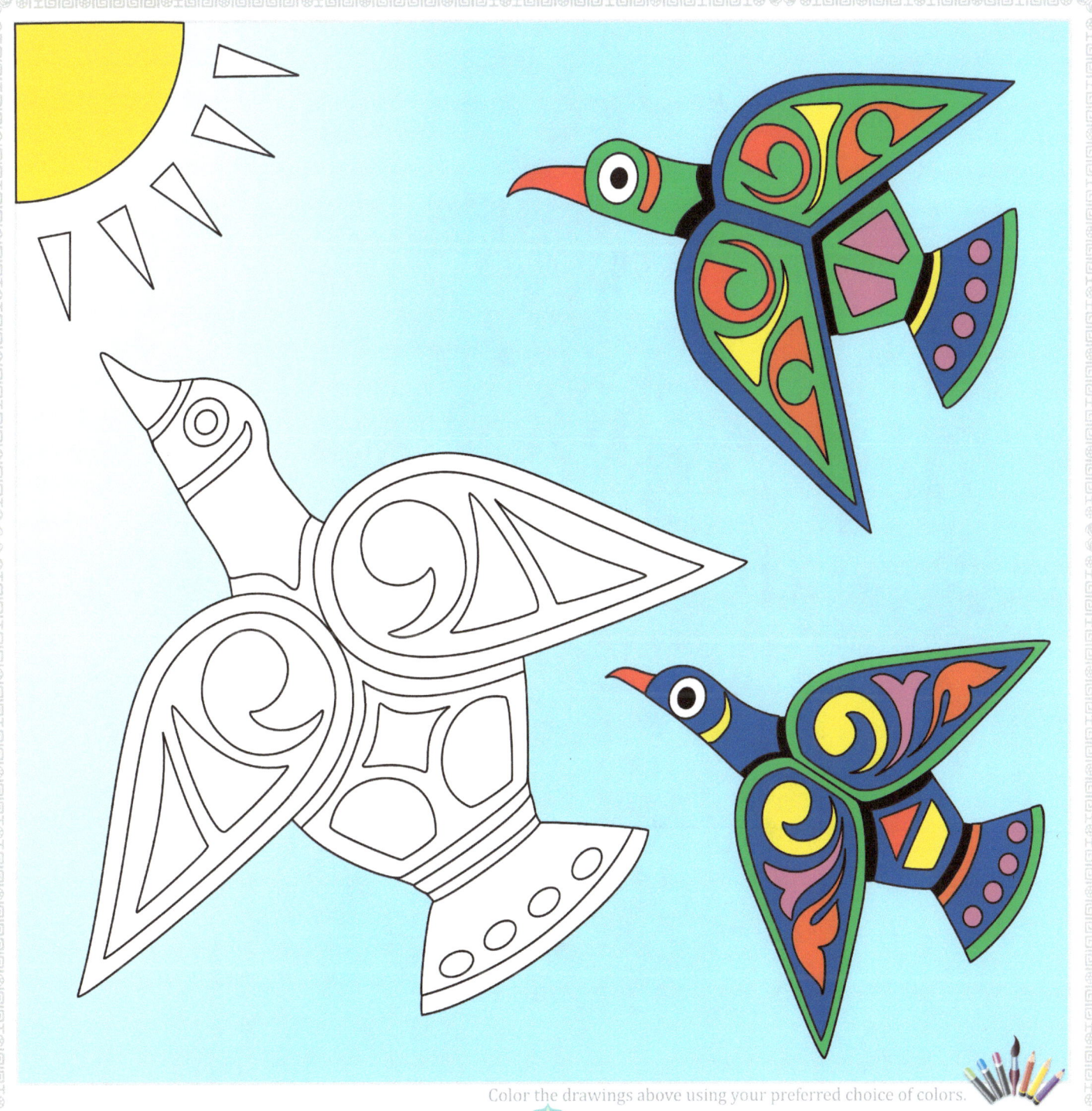

Color the drawings above using your preferred choice of colors.

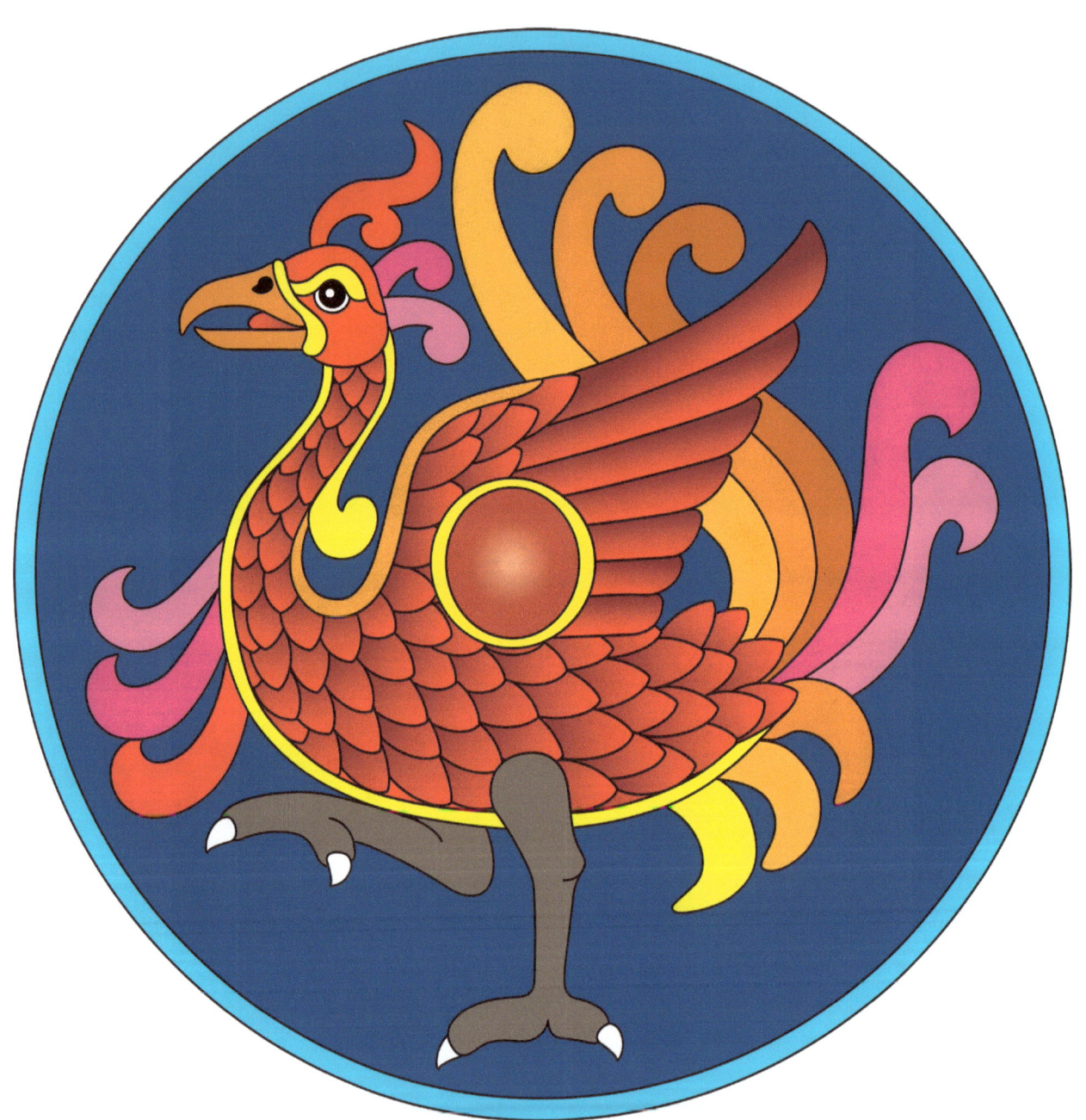

The Red Bird is the symbol of the South. Han Dynasty, 206 B.C.E. - 221 C.E.

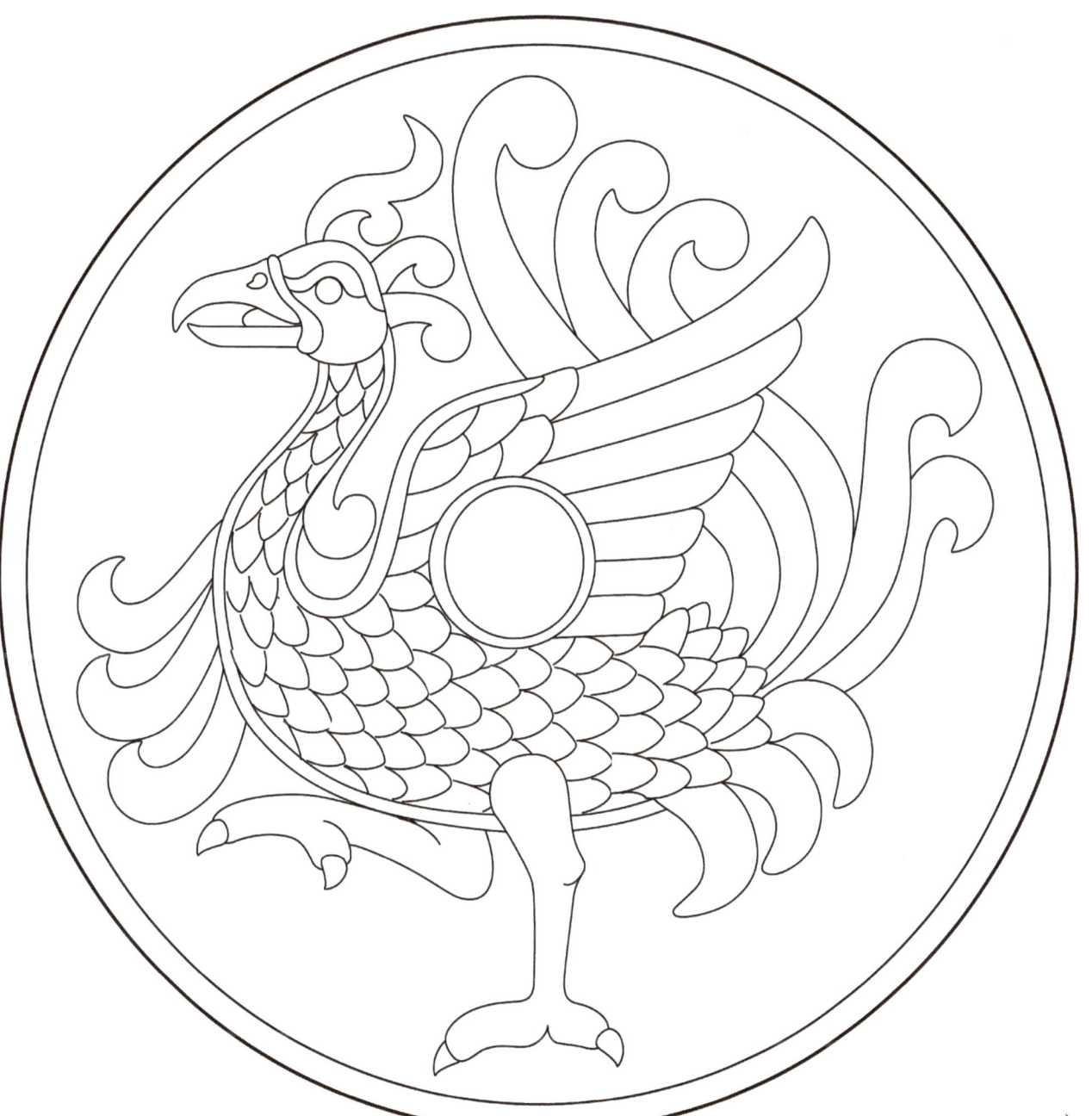

Color the drawing above using your preferred choice of colors.

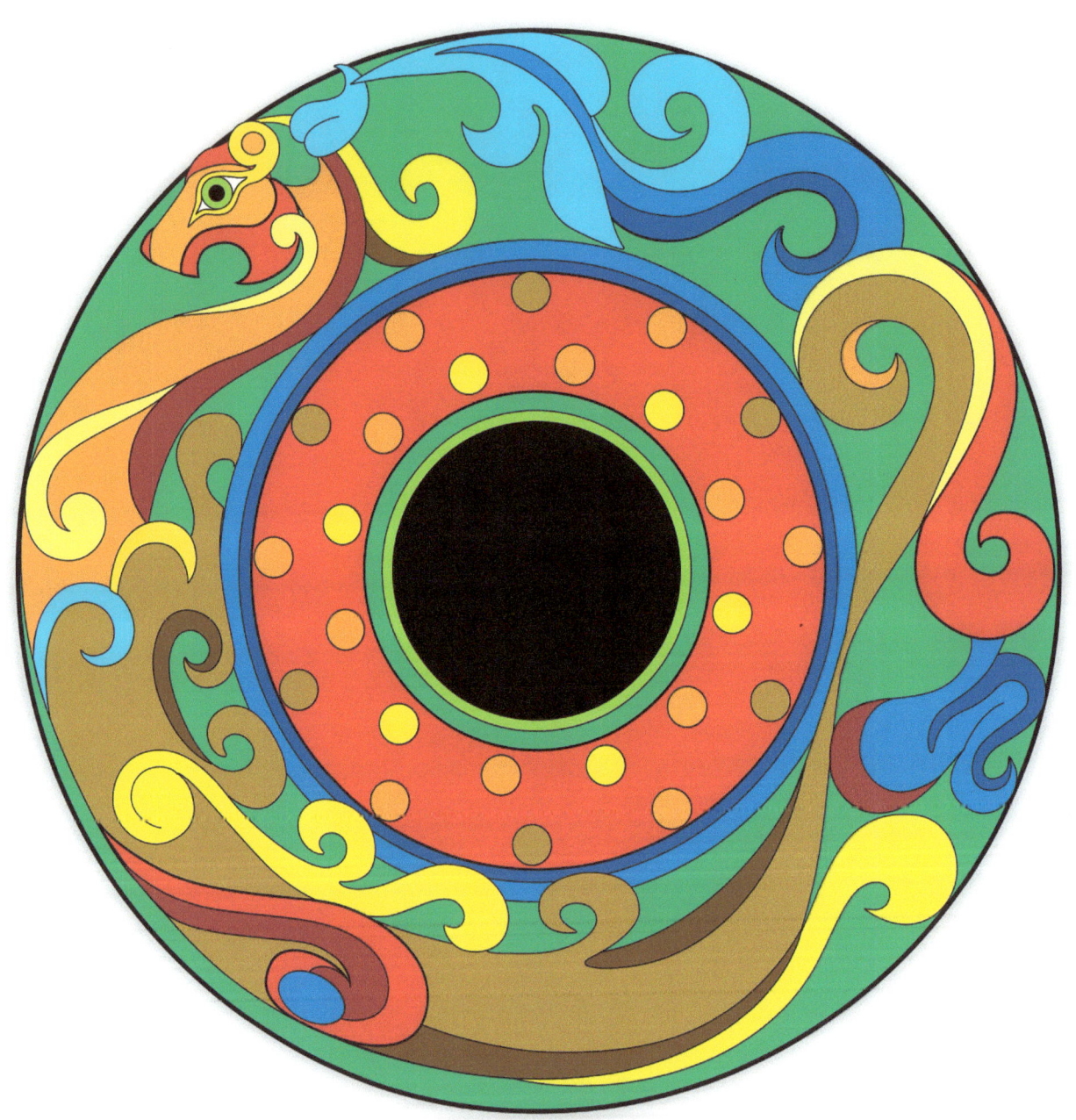

A concentric "Huan" Disc, decorated with dragons.
Warring States Period, 475 B.C.E. - 221 B.C.E.

Color the drawing above using your preferred choice of colors.

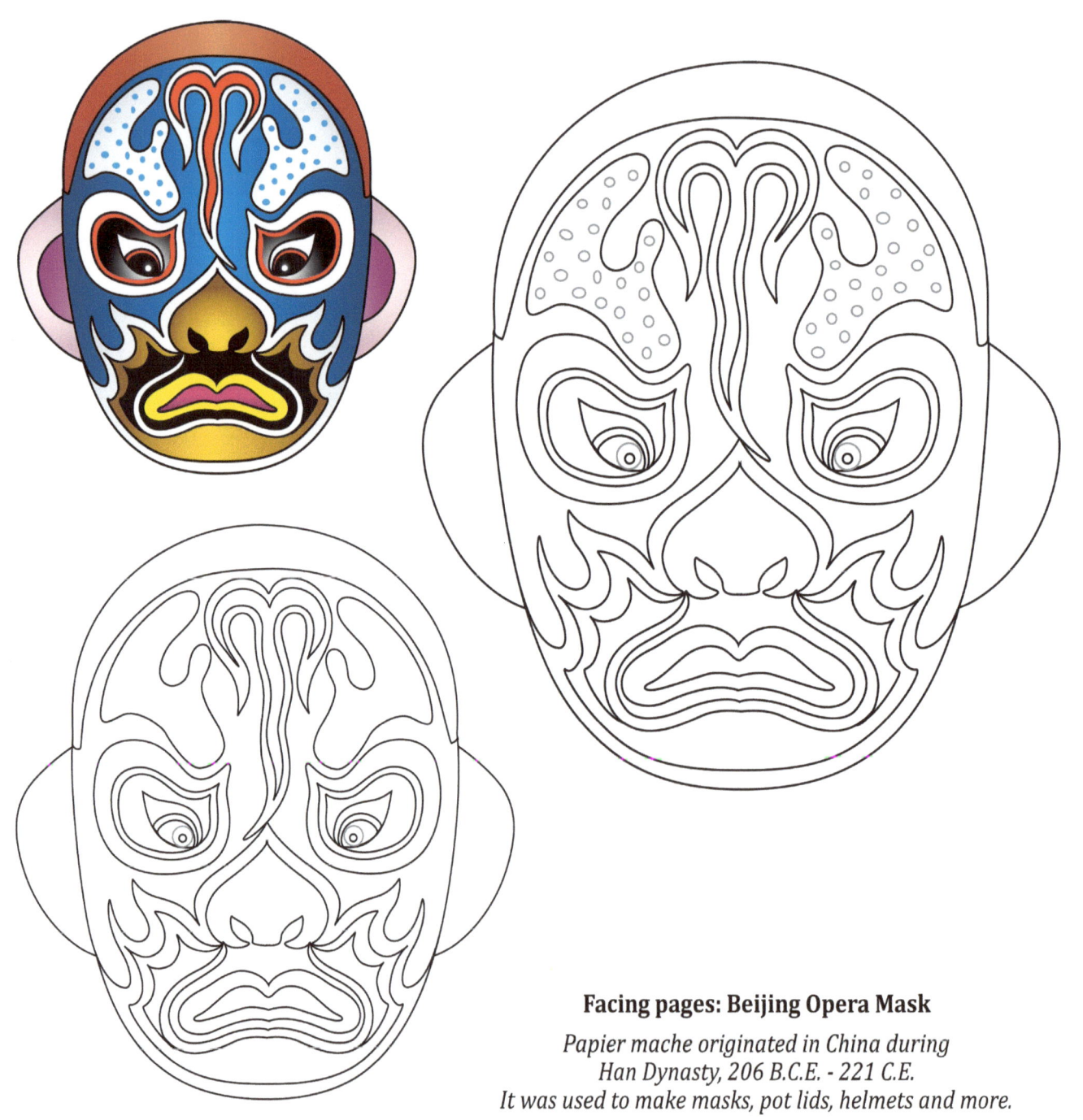

Facing pages: Beijing Opera Mask

*Papier mache originated in China during
Han Dynasty, 206 B.C.E. - 221 C.E.
It was used to make masks, pot lids, helmets and more.*

Color the drawings above using your preferred choice of colors.

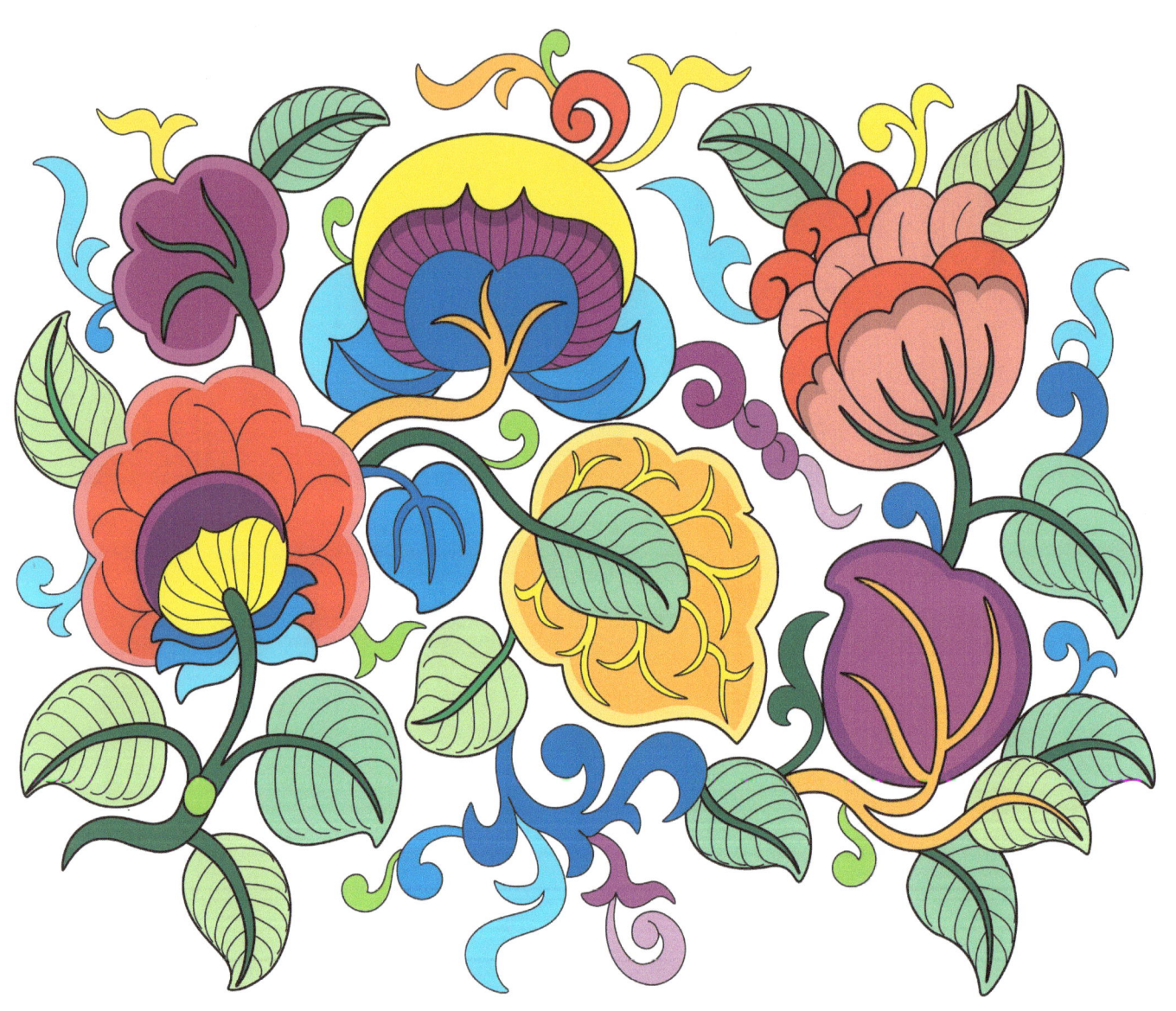

*Floral drawing with peonies on a covered jar. The decoration
was traced in beaten silver, usually given as a gift. Tang Dynasty, 618 C.E. - 907 C.E.*

Color the drawing above using your preferred choice of colors.

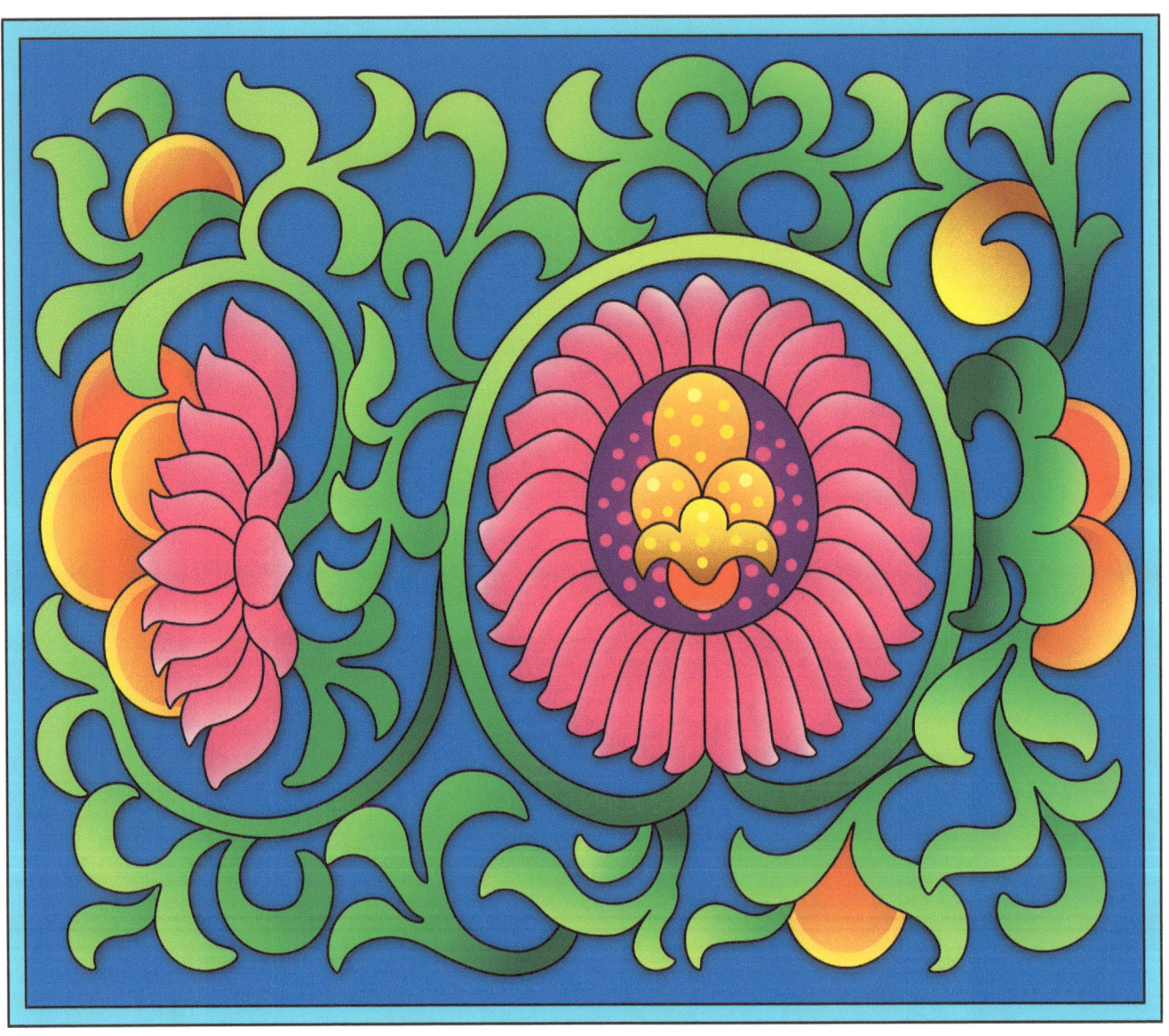

*Floral decorating designs from a light
glaze to a darker slip on a pitcher. Northern Song Dynasty, 960 C.E. - 1127 C.E.*

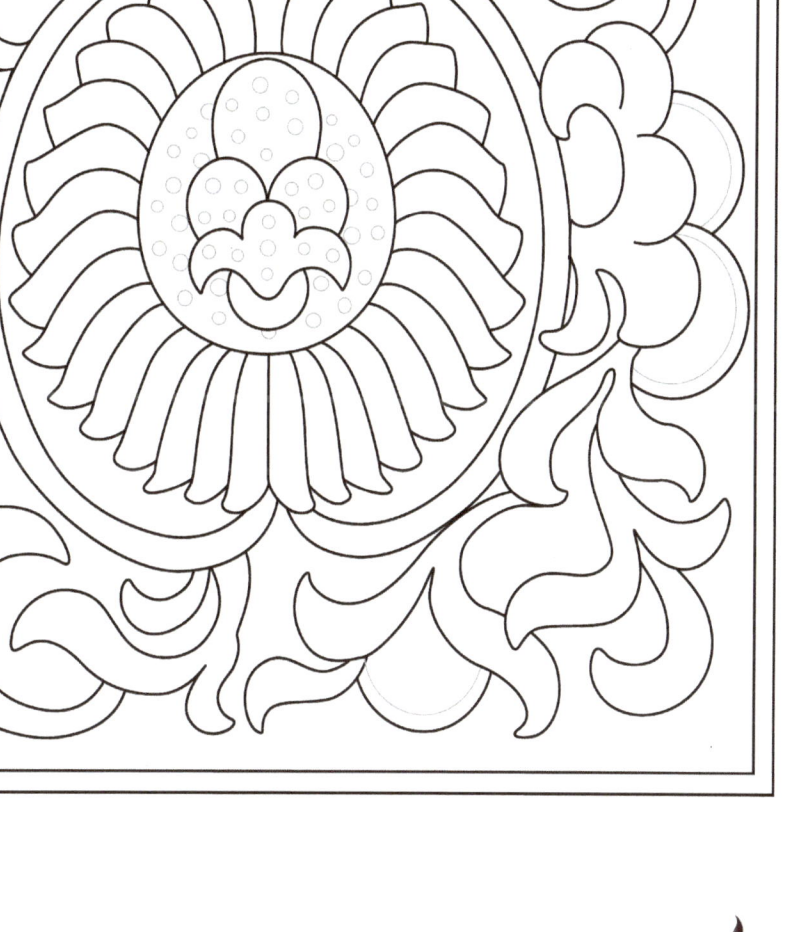

Color the drawing above using your preferred choice of colors.

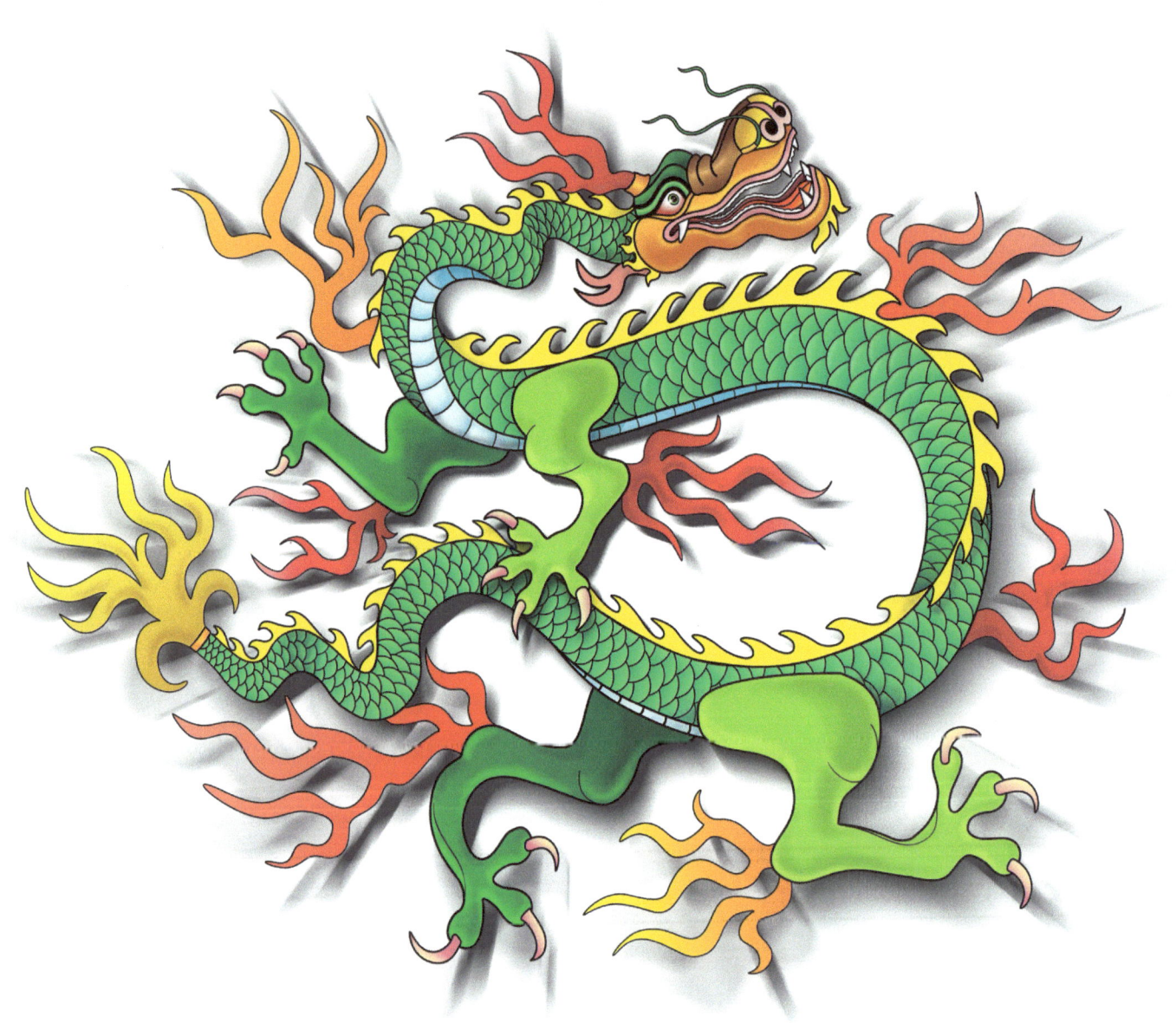

Dragon, from a Chinese porcelain. Ming Dynasty, 1368 C.E. - 1644 C.E.

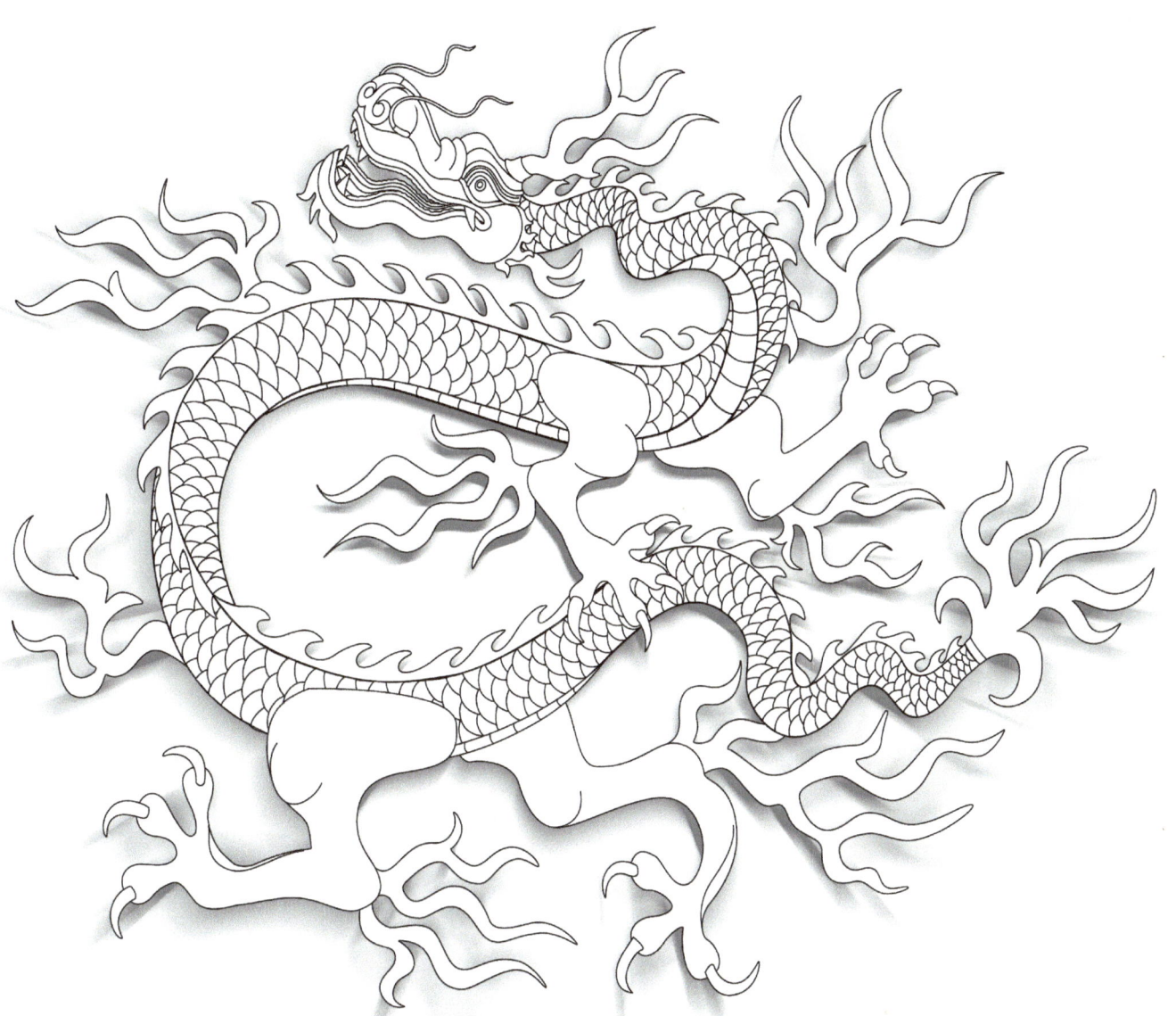

Color the drawing above using your preferred choice of colors.

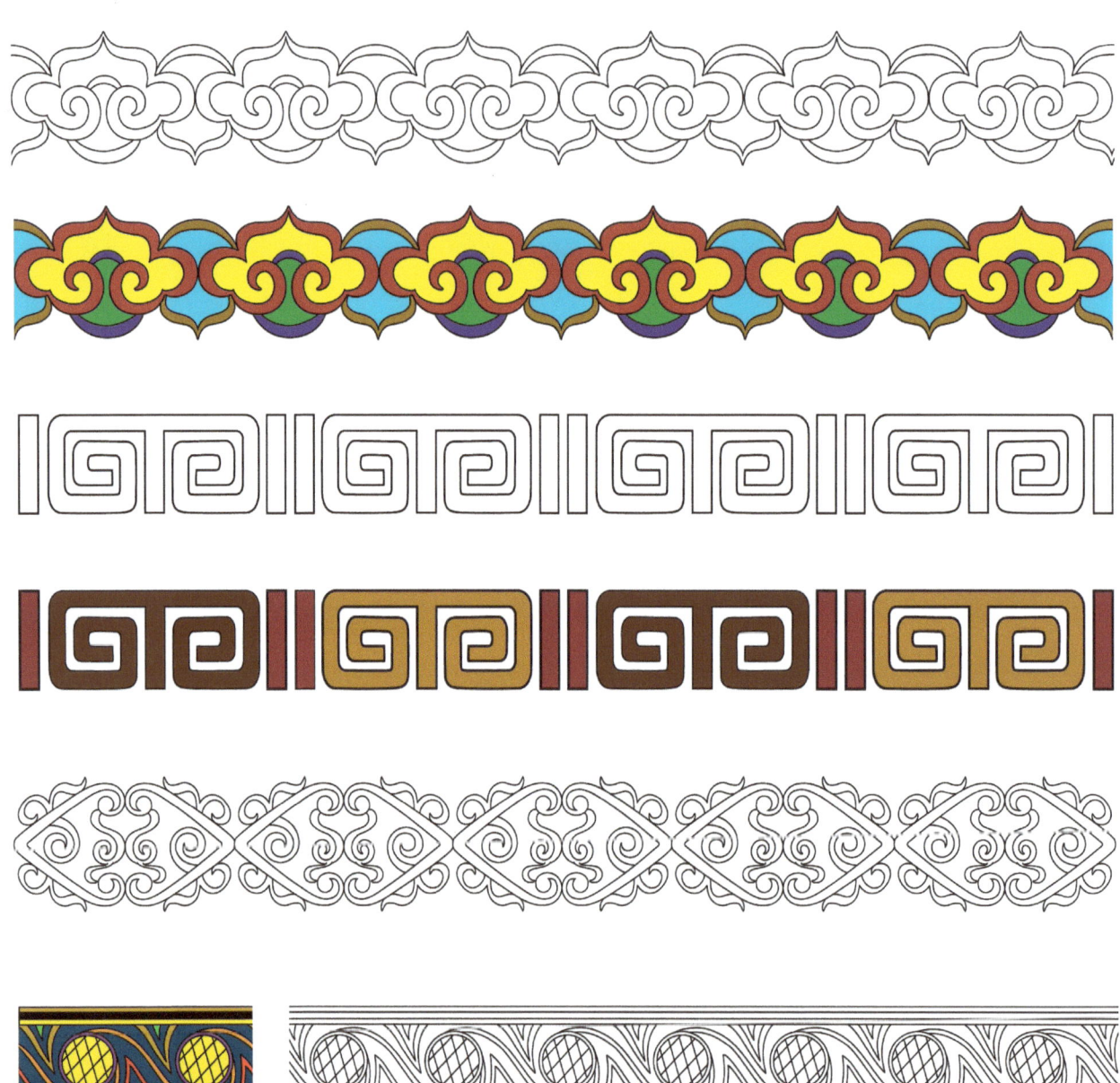

Using these images as examples, create your own piece using the elements found in Chinese Art.

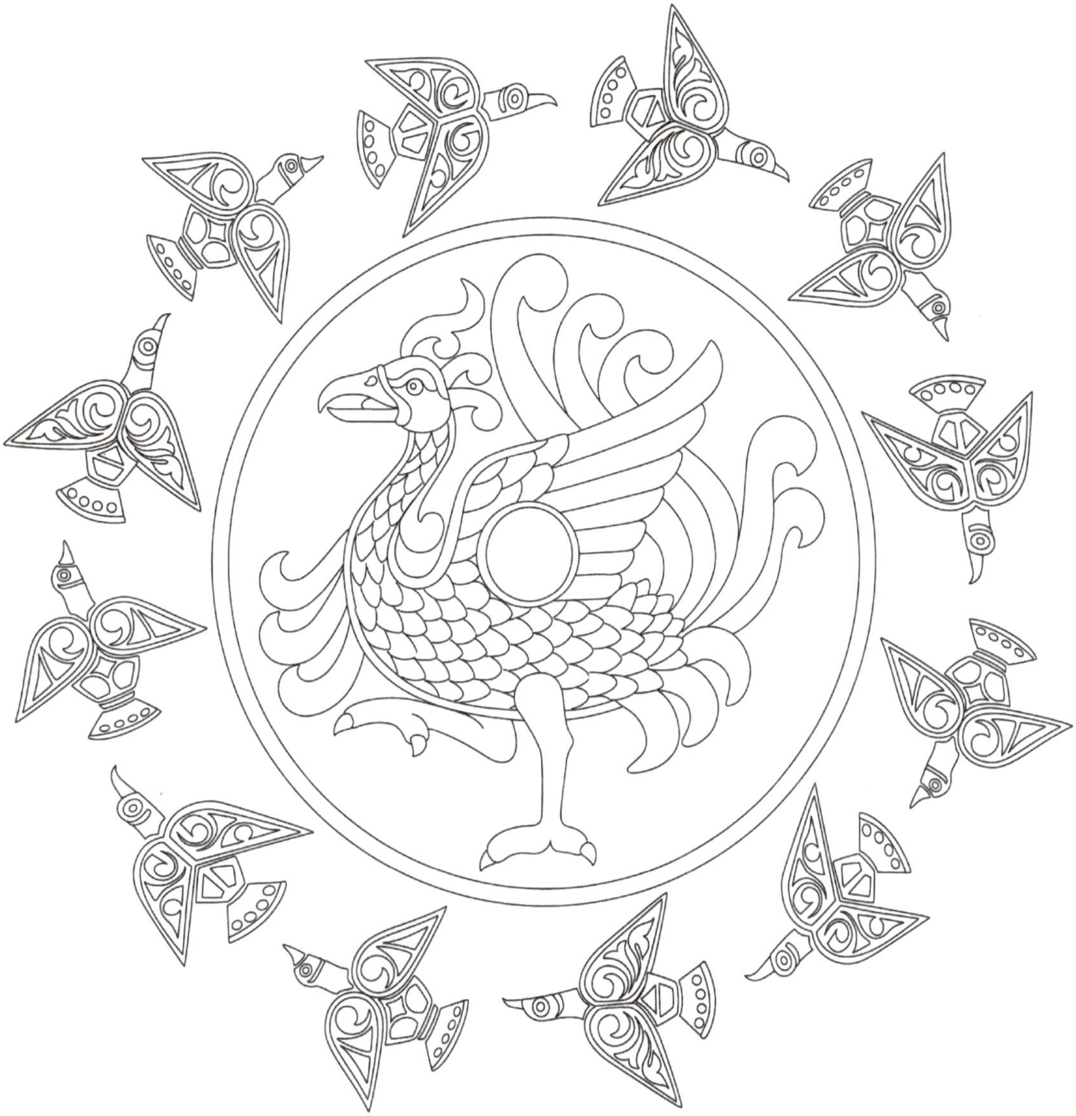

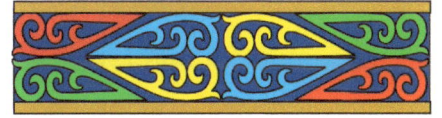

Color the drawings above using your preferred choice of colors.

= a synopsis of =
Chinese Art

Chinese Art during the early Stone Age consisted of pottery and sculptures, which dates back to as early as 10,000 B.C.E., and is still inarguably one of the oldest tradition of art in the world. It is often classified by the succession of the Chinese emperors, most of which have lasted hundreds of years.

The fundamentals of a Chinese painting consisted of six principals, which were: First, creating a life-like tone and atmosphere; Second, building structures through brushwork; Third, depicting the forms and things as they are; Fourth, applying appropriate coloring; Fifth, composition; and finally the Sixth, which was transcribing and copying.

Traditional ink wash paintings were practiced by scholar-officials. The landscape was developed as aesthetic values dependent on the imagination of the artist. Artists painted human figures from the Han period (206 B.C.E. - 221 C.E.) to the Tang Dynasties (618 C.E. - 907 C.E.). They preserved paintings on silk banners, lacquered objects, and even on tomb walls. From the Five Dynasties to the Northern Song era (960 C.E. - 1127 C.E.) it is known as, 'The Golden age of Chinese Landscapes.'

Decorative art is vital among the traditional Chinese art. Over the years, countless fine works produced in various imperial factories by Chinese artists in the form of porcelain, textile and so forth. Chinese ceramic ware was continuously developed since the predynastic periods as a significant form of Chinese art. Chinese jade was attributed with magical powers and was used both in the Stone and Bronze ages for large weapons, tools, and vessels.

Like paintings, calligraphy was also deeply appreciated in China. Chinese amateurs, aristocrats, and scholar-officials made the time to perfect the technique and gain the necessary sensibility for calligraphic brushwork. Calligraphy was thought to be the highest and purest form of painting. Wang Xizhe was a famous Chinese Calligrapher and lived in the 4th Century B.C.E.

OTHER TITLES IN THIS SERIES

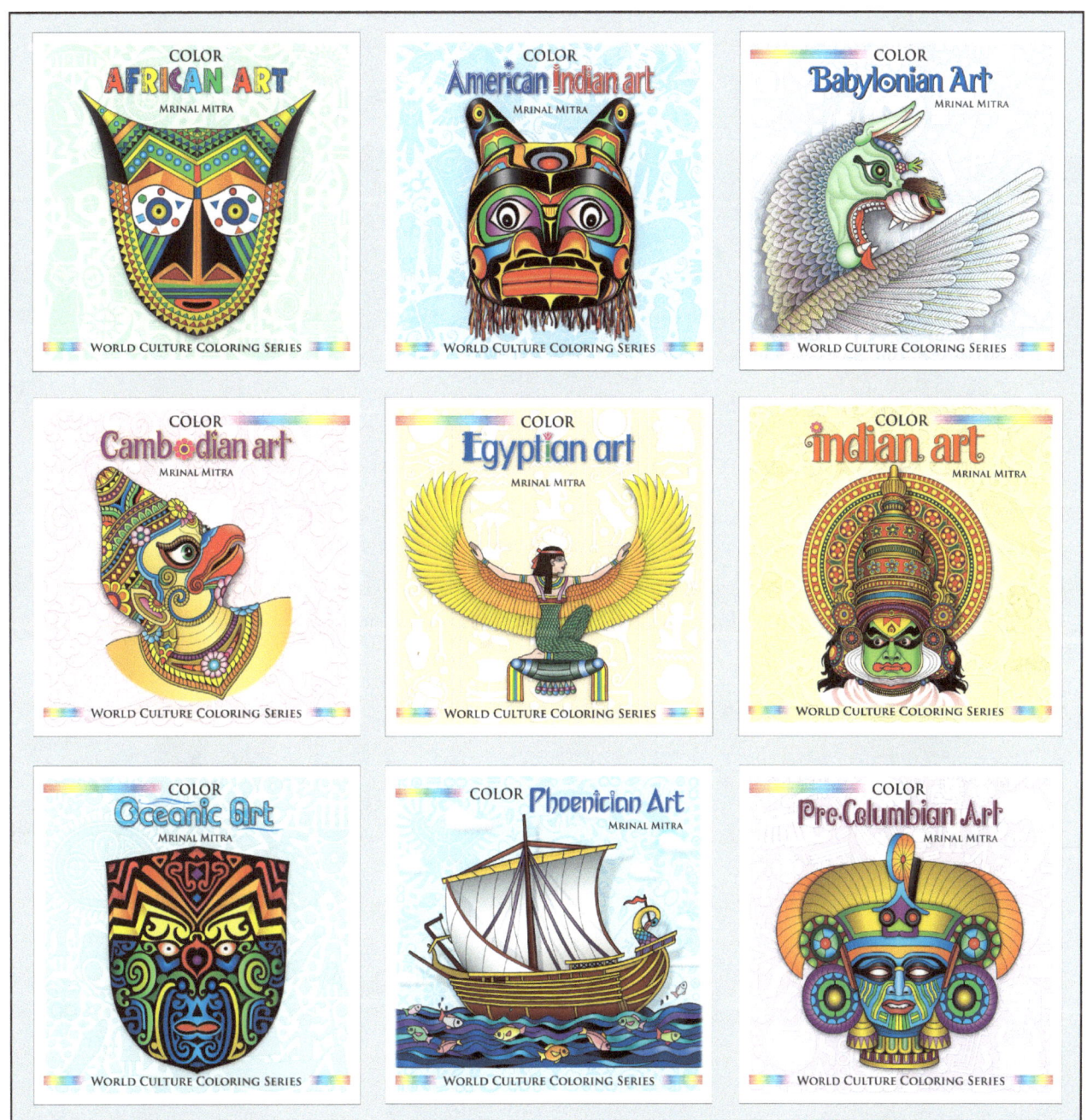

COLOR
AFRICAN ART
MRINAL MITRA
WORLD CULTURE COLORING SERIES

COLOR
American Indian art
MRINAL MITRA
WORLD CULTURE COLORING SERIES

COLOR
Babylonian Art
MRINAL MITRA
WORLD CULTURE COLORING SERIES

COLOR
Cambodian art
MRINAL MITRA
WORLD CULTURE COLORING SERIES

COLOR
Egyptian art
MRINAL MITRA
WORLD CULTURE COLORING SERIES

COLOR
Indian art
MRINAL MITRA
WORLD CULTURE COLORING SERIES

COLOR
Oceanic Art
MRINAL MITRA
WORLD CULTURE COLORING SERIES

COLOR **Phoenician Art**
MRINAL MITRA
WORLD CULTURE COLORING SERIES

COLOR
Pre-Columbian Art
MRINAL MITRA
WORLD CULTURE COLORING SERIES

AVAILABLE FROM AMAZON.COM, CREATESPACE.COM, AND OTHER RETAIL OUTLETS

Acknowledgement

First and foremost, this series would not be possible without the number of great historical art found within the different cultural regions around the world.

In addition, we would like to acknowledge the variety of publishing's from all over the world for allowing us to learn about their fascinating ancestral art and culture. With this provided knowledge, we have hoped to have represented the art as splendidly as you have supplied it.

About the Author

Mrinal Mitra has earned a number of prestigious awards, both Indian and International, and received honors for his outstanding illustrations. Some of his recognitions include; The Noma Concours Award, Japan (twice), Illustrators Award, and Children's Choice Award, India, and honors from German Television "Transtel", BRNO- CSSR, TIBI- Iran, and UNICEF, New York.

Many of his talented artworks have been exhibited in several different countries such as; India, Japan, Italy, Czech Republic, Iran, and New Zealand. Mitra has authored, designed and illustrated trade and educational children's books for many Indian as well as Multinational Book Publishers around the globe.

Copyright: Mrinal Mitra, 2014

Printed by CreateSpace, An Amazon.com. Company
Available from Amazon.com, CreateSpace.com, and other retail outlets

For further inquiry please contact Mrinal Mitra at: mitra_mrinal@hotmail.com